And

# MORAL
# DEVELOPMENT,
# ETHICS
# AND FAITH

Translated by Kenneth C. Russell

**NOVALIS**

*For fellow travellers*
*Rosaire Bellemare,*
*Jacques L'heureux*
*and Achiel Peelman.*

Layout and design: Gilles Lépine

Front cover: "Crouching Boy" by Michaelangelo. About 1525.
Leningrad, Hermitage

Translation: Kenneth C. Russell

© 1992 Novalis, Saint Paul University,
Ottawa, Ontario, Canada

Business Office:
Novalis, P.O. Box 990, Outremont, Quebec
H2V 4S7, Canada

Legal Deposit: 1st trimester 1992, National Library of Canada and
Bibliothèque Nationale du Québec

ISBN 2-89088-533-X

Printed in Canada

**Canadian Cataloguing in Publication Data**

Guindon, André, 1933-

Moral development, ethics and faith

Translation of: Le développement moral

Includes bibliographical references

ISBN 2-89088-533-X

1. Moral development. I. Title

BF723.M54G8313     1992     155.2'34     C92-090075-5

# Contents

# Preface

Whenever the government is debating a bill involving moral values such as the legal status of homosexual acts, capital punishment or abortion, the television screen bombards us with daily reports on the positions taken by people who claim to be spokespersons for this or that group on the right, left or in the centre, with round tables of so–called experts, and with public opinion polls, each claiming to be more scientific than the rest. While sitting back listening to the debate, we may at times be surprised to find ourselves on the same wavelength as someone maintaining a position different from our own. At other times we may find it difficult to listen to the presentation of someone defending arguments with which we substantially agree.

Where does this dichotomy between agreement on specific issues and disagreement on the mode of ethical discourse come from? There are many plausible explanations: similarity or dissimilarity in terms of education, socioeconomic class, religious affiliation or ethnic origin, or the influences of the surrounding culture. These factors, however, are not always decisive. Why do the arguments of some Brazilian from a *favela* in Rio de Janeiro, supporting a certain kind of violent intervention that I consider unjust or ill–advised, seem worth listening to, while I can hardly stand the remarks of my colleague, who agrees with me that this is not the right way to proceed?

The American psychologist, Lawrence Kohlberg, and the researchers he has trained, have shed light on this question by continuing the kind of research begun by the Swiss scholar, Jean Piaget, who first published his findings in 1932. Using extensive empirical data they have shown that our disputes about ethics take shape against one or another of the backdrops that humanity holds in common in its quest for meaning. These researchers argue that each of us is able to construct six of these moral backdrops in a set sequence of stages over the span of a lifetime. These moral backdrops furnish no specific solutions to the dilemmas we face, but they do provide an internal structure which harmonizes all the judgments and choices we make. Irrespective of the positions two people take, their at least implicit recognition of a common backdrop allows them to understand each other.

I have three goals in writing this book. First of all, I want to make the theories about the stages of moral development and the results of research on which they are based more widely known. Secondly, I want to suggest that some of the major western ethical models basically reflect a specific stage of moral development. Finally, by underlining what is at stake in each model, I want to show how they affect our secular and religious commitments.

# Introduction

## Research into Moral Development

Towards the end of his undergraduate studies, a youthful Jean Piaget (1896–1980) decided that the philosophical theories which try to explain human understanding lack a solid experimental base. When he joined the J. J. Rousseau Institute in Geneva in 1921 he resolved to put an end to this state of affairs and to consecrate "two or three years" to the study of how children think. This was to give him the experimental knowledge he needed to elaborate a genetic epistemology. He had no idea that he would dedicate more than 50 years of his life to this study, and that he would become the leader of the influential constructive–developmental school of cognitive psychology.[1]

To decipher completely the mystery of the cognitive mechanism's structures, Piaget extended his research to the

---

[1]    B. Inhelder and J. Piaget, *The Growth of Logical Thinking from Childhood to Adolescence: An Essay on the Construction of Formal Operational Structures* (New York: Basic Books, 1958); J. Piaget and B. Inhelder, *The Psychology of the Child* (New York: Basic Books, 1969).

area of moral reasoning. With the help of a team of gifted collaborators, he applied a new clinical method, partly verbal and partly concrete, that used play and short stories. He tried to understand how children interpret rules and moral concepts. At the end of this study Piaget stated that, around five or six years of age, his subjects pass from a stage of anomie, where they have no sense of moral law, to a stage of moral heteronomy, where they demonstrate a unilateral respect for, and obedience to, the rules set by those older than themselves. Around eight to 10 years of age, the co-operation they have learned allows them to move towards the stage of moral autonomy they achieve when they are about 13 or 14. They have, then, established a morality of mutual respect for rationally worked out rules.[2] Piaget laid the cornerstone of modern moral development research. He did not, however, follow up his studies in morals. Nonetheless, his work on the four stages of the development of logical thought continues to influence research in moral development.

A young American, Lawrence Kohlberg (1928–1987), took up the torch a quarter of a century later. He told short fictional stories posing a moral dilemma to a sampling of 84 boys, aged 10, 13 and 16, from the Chicago area. For example, does Heinz have the right to steal a medication to save the life of his wife if he has no other means to procure it, or should he respect the property rights of the druggist?[3]

---

[2]  J. Piaget, *The Moral Judgment of the Child* (New York: The Free Press, 1965).

[3]  L. Kohlberg, "The Development of Modes of Moral Thinking and Choice in the Years Ten to Sixteen" (unpublished doctoral dissertation, University of Chicago, 1958), p. 69–75.

Then he asked them how those involved should solve their dilemma. From the moral protocols he collected, Kohlberg learned that the passage from heteronomy (subjection to someone else's law) to autonomy (subjection to a self-imposed law) is more complex and slower than Piaget had indicated. He proposed a new interpretation of Piaget's stages. There are, he argued, three moral levels, each comprising two distinct stages. The sequence of moral development may be laid out as follows:

Level I: Preconventional

   Stage 1: Heteronomy: Punishment/Obedience

   Stage 2: Instrumental Purpose and Exchange

Level II: Conventional

   Stage 3: Interpersonal Expectations

   Stage 4: Social System

Level III: Postconventional

   Stage 5: Social Contract

   Stage 6: Universal Ethical Principles[4]

At regular intervals Kohlberg visited 50 of his original subjects and collected their answers to the same "case of conscience" that he had posed to them when they were 10,

---

[4]    Kohlberg's major studies can be found in *Essays on Moral Development* (San Francisco: Harper and Row, 1981–1984). For the latest revision of the manual used by the Kohlberg school, see A. Colby and others, *The Measurement of Moral Judgment: A Manual and Its Results* (New York: Cambridge University Press, 1983). The current positions of the school are presented and defended in L. Kohlberg, C. Levine and A. Hewer, *Moral Stages: A Current Formulation and a Response to Critics* (Basel: S. Karger, 1983).

13 or 16 years old. A research team soon gathered around him at Harvard University's School of Education and collected additional moral protocols from both male and female subjects of all ages.

In 1973 he announced that the sequence went beyond adolescence, and reinterpreted its meaning.[5] The work of refining the research tools, the scoring of the protocols, the interpretation of the results, and the precise delineation of the field of research continues. Today there are more than 2,000 Kohlbergian research reports. Despite the various criticisms levelled against it, this school continues to lead the field. It exercises considerable influence on faculties of education, not only in the United States and Canada, but in many other countries.[6]

## The Hard Stages of the Kohlberg School

Kohlberg, like other competent scientific researchers, knows the precise boundaries that define what he is isolating and measuring. Contrary to what many popularizers and educators think, Kohlberg is not describing moral development *per se*. He focusses on one aspect only: how the subject reasons about impersonal and hypothetical dilemmas concerning justice. Kohlberg has nothing to say about

---

[5]    L. Kohlberg, "Continuities in Childhood and Adult Moral Development Revisited," in P. B. Baltes and K. W. Schaie (eds.), *Life Span Development Psychology: Personality and Socialization* (New York: Academic Press, 1973), pp. 179–204.

[6]    For a review of the research on Kohlberg's major positions, see L. J. Walker, "Cognitive Processes in Moral Development," in G. L. Sapp (ed.), *Handbook of Moral Development: Models, Processes, Techniques, and Research* (Birmingham: Religious Education Press, 1986), pp. 109–145.

the other components of moral development. Consecutive editions of the *Scoring Manual* warn interviewers to ignore their subjects' system of values or their motivations for willing the good. The only point of interest is their normative ethics, i.e., the way in which they conceive the conflict of rights, and how they determine moral obligations. No interest is taken in their meta–ethics.

Kohlberg also abstracts from the conscious or unconscious affective elements influencing his subjects' moral judgments. He pays no attention whatsoever to the connections between the judgments they make concerning the hypothetical case and those they work out in daily life. Consequently, he ignores the links that connect judgment and action, knowledge and free will, conviction and responsibility. In regard to dilemmas involving, for example, personal rules of sexual integration and the manifestation of courage and concern for others, he has no idea whether or not his subjects are reasoning in the same way they do when faced with dilemmas involving the conflict of rights and social demands. He deliberately wants to leave aside all but the purely logical aspects of the knowledge at work in moral discernment. Except for some research on how the community to which the subjects belong influences their normative judgments, Kohlberg pays no attention to any possible environmental pressures. Obviously, this reductionism fits a Socratic or idealist notion of morality better than an Aristotelian or realist conception. Kohlberg identifies himself with the idealist ethical tradition.[7]

---

[7]    L. Kohlberg, "Education for Justice: A Modern Statement of the Platonic View," in J. W. Gustafson and others, *Five Lectures* (Cambridge: Harvard University Press, 1970), pp. 57–83.

Kohlberg's focus on only one variable of the sequence does not invalidate his research in any way. On the contrary, its scientific value rests on this rigorous delimitation of the object under investigation. Kohlberg's careful examination of the normative judgments of his subjects shows that, no matter what obligations these proclaim, they reason about moral obligations in six distinct ways; that these reasoning structures always follow one another in the same sequential order, without regression and without any stages ever being skipped; that each higher stage represents the adoption of a more inclusive moral perspective than the preceding; that this sequence is so universal that it is just as much in evidence among the Inuit of Alaska as it is among the kibbutzniks of Israel, among women as among men, among agnostics as among believers. The only differences worth noting concern the rate of development, which is generally faster in urban than in traditional settings, and among the upper and middle social classes than among the less privileged.

Kohlberg and his colleagues warn us that scoring the moral protocol of a subject at a lower level of development does not mean that this individual is less concerned with moral rectitude than someone scored at a higher level. There is even less justification for the presumption that this individual will behave improperly. The major consequence of the existence of a sequence of development is that more advanced subjects have a sharper sense of what looks fair to someone else. We owe it to others to grasp correctly the point of view that they take when they make a normative judgment. Their operative notion of good and evil (which is not necessarily conceptualized and defined, but which, nonetheless, serves to determine moral obligations) is not ours. Consequently, if we establish our own moral judgments on the basis of a pattern of reasoning that others have not yet constructed, they may agree with our judgment without, however, grasping the validity of the arguments we put forward.

Like Piaget's stages of logical thought, Kohlberg's are presented as structured cognitive wholes. Each stage represents a form that intelligence assumes for a longer or shorter period of time, or even permanently, during its development. In different ways the studies of Piaget and Kohlberg furnish criteria to establish that a way of thinking logically or morally should be classified as a stage.[8]

The stages which verify these criteria are currently called "hard stages." In the cognitive–development approach the stages do not, then, represent a period of life in which the subjects have such and such needs, emphasize such and such motivations, or invest themselves with such and such psychic power. They represent a cognitive interaction between subject and object and the particular way in which subjects perceive their world. Each stage designates a logical–moral construct with its own consistency and internal coherence.

Can Kohlberg really insist that his subjects do not regress to a lower stage? To use concrete cases of regressive reasoning, as people often do in opposing him, shows that they have not understood the narrow range of Kohlberg's position. He limits himself to insisting that once subjects put together a new structure of moral reasoning, they never

---

[8]    See J. Piaget, *Structuralism* (New York: Harper & Row, 1970), pp. 3–16; L. Kohlberg, C. Levine and A. Hewer, *Moral Stages: A Current Formulation and a Response to Critics*, p. 31.

lose what they have firmly grasped. Whether subjects, who have reached the proficiency of stage 5, use this form of reasoning in this or that situation is another question altogether. Whatever form of reasoning they use, and whatever solution they come to, they are always capable of appreciating the logic of a stage 5 moral judgment.[9]

## Towards a Theory of Soft Stages

The scientific community was not inactive while Kohlberg was pursuing his research into what he called, metonymically, "moral development." In 1963, shortly after Kohlberg questioned his Chicago boys, Norman Bull, an English educator, undertook a more ambitious research project that ran until 1967 and involved 360 boys and girls, aged seven to 17.[10] His methods of inquiry were also more diversified than those of his predecessors. He used written tests, visual materials and personal interviews. Drawing, like Kohlberg, on Piaget's research, he ended up with four stages. He introduced the stage of socionomy (around eight to 11 years of age), after anomie and heteronomy, to replace Piaget's semi–autonomous stage.

Bull's criticisms of Piaget's interpretations of the evidence miss the mark, however, because he does not have a "hard" notion of the stages. He fails to grasp the constructivism of Piaget's approach. His stages follow along side by side instead of being integrated into one another. Even

---

9    C. G. Levine, "Stage Acquisition and Stage Use: An Appraisal of Stage Displacement Explanations of Variation in Moral Reasoning," *Human Development,* Vol. 22, 1979, pp. 145–164.

10    N. J. Bull, *Moral Judgement from Childhood to Adolescence* (London: Routledge and Kegan Paul, 1969).

though the cognitive factor remains the real key to human development, many other psychological, educational, socioeconomic and religious elements, as well as the variations introduced by sex, are considered. Although the results are interesting, the lack of control over these variables compromises their value.

The American disciples of Piaget's approach have been more cautious. They have not ignored the plethora of sequential schemes of development that the representatives of the various psychological schools have proposed. Books like *Ego Development,* by Jane Loevinger of Boston University, have taken on the task of keeping them on the alert.[11] In addition to proposing her own sequence, Loevinger lists the various sequences, including Piaget's, Kohlberg's and Bull's, and lines them up in a number of comparative tables. These comparisons displeased Kohlberg, who wanted to keep his sequence uncontaminated by considerations of the self's psychodynamic states.[12] Nonetheless, this paralleling of sequences makes it evident that Kohlberg's moral sequence resembles those of his competitors. They all show a progressive expansion of the subjects' perspective, and a progressive liberation from the factors which interfere with their vision of the world and their involvement in it.

Kohlberg's resistance to premature alliances has forced his disciples to become methodologically critical. Some of them, nonetheless, realize that an approach to moral devel-

---

[11] J. Loevinger, *Ego Development* (San Francisco: Jossey–Bass, 1976).

[12] L. Kohlberg, *The Meaning and Measure of Moral Development* (Worchester: Clark University Press, 1981).

opment that refuses to consider variables, other than the mode of reasoning, lacks long-term interest. Even at Harvard, therefore, they are beginning to break Kohlberg's taboo against considering any but purely cognitive factors in moral development.

Carol Gilligan, a close associate of Kohlberg, has initiated a research project comparing samples of men and women. She is also comparing the answers her subjects give to Kohlberg's hypothetical dilemmas with their answers to personal moral dilemmas. Gilligan's results suggest that her female subjects opt for a caring rather than a justice model. Especially at the postconventional level, Kohlberg's sequence misrepresents how the majority of women, and a limited number of men, reason.[13] Gilligan shatters a restrictive concept of Kohlberg's ethics.

While he was still teaching at Harvard Divinity School, James Fowler followed Kohlberg's work very closely. His own theological concerns have prompted him to examine the human structures of faith's development.[14] Fowler, who adopts Kohlberg's sequence, baptizes the six stages and gives them a broader interpretation. This has turned out to be a valuable contribution. On the one hand, Fowler has guaranteed his structural–developmental orthodoxy by measuring, like Piaget, the logical competency of his subjects and, like Kohlberg, their moral ability. On the other hand, he has added other structural characteristics to the

---

13    C. Gilligan, *In a Different Voice: Psychological Theory and Women's Development* (Cambridge: Harvard University Press, 1982).

14    J. W. Fowler, "Life/Faith Patterns: Structures of Trust and Loyalty," in J. Berryman (ed.), *Life Maps: Conversation on the Journey of Faith* (Waco: Winston Press, 1978), pp. 14–101.

stages: form of world–coherence, locus of authority, limits of social awareness and role of symbols. Fowler clearly articulates the social aspects of both Piaget's conception of morality as a form of respect for social rules, and Kohlberg's as a cognitive, interactional ability (role–taking) in the resolution of social conflicts. But, by exploring the metaphysical and symbolic aspects of cognition, he has helped to broaden the excessively rationalistic conception that his masters held. He has also paid attention to religious knowledge which, sociologists point out, plays an essential role in the construction of social reality by structuring the perceptions of the subjects.[15] This goes beyond Kohlberg who, instead of reflecting on this phenomenon at each stage of development, relegated it to a seventh quasi–stage.[16]

The most recent contribution of Kohlberg's disciples comes from Robert Kegan.[17] He dedicates his book to "the living legacy of Jean Piaget." The adjective "living" is important. In fact, Kegan offers a fresh reading of Piaget's major insights into the structures by which human subjects adapt to their environment. He also provides an intelligible framework that is large enough to integrate the psychodynamic tradition of the ages of the life of the self into Kohlberg's sequence of development. Kegan, like all the reformers of the Kohlberg school, turns towards Erik

---

[15] P. L. Berger and T. Luckman, *The Social Construction of Reality: A Treatise in the Sociology of Knowledge* (Garden City: Doubleday, 1966).

[16] F. C. Power and L. Kohlberg, "Religion, Morality, and Ego Develoment," in C. Brusselman and others, *Toward Moral and Religious Maturity* (Morristown: Silver Burdett, 1980), pp. 344–372.

[17] R. Kegan, *The Evolving Self: Problem and Process in Human Development* (Cambridge: Harvard University Press, 1982).

Erikson to explore the more obscure aspects of the epigenesis of self–identity.[18]

In opposition to the "hard" stages of Kohlbergian orthodoxy, the stages of Gilligan, Fowler, Kegan and others are labelled "soft."[19] This does not imply, however, that these approaches are simple–minded. We are not dealing with the methodological failure to differentiate for which Norman Bull was chided. All the recent authors have employed the structuralist method of Piaget's stages. They have all done their best to respect the spirit, if not the letter, of Piaget's criteria. But their description of development includes non–rational factors which are not logically necessary. Introducing these into a sequence that continues to be conditioned by the cognitive structures, leaves room for the human freedom Piaget's concept fails to recognize.

When I describe the stages of moral development in the following pages, I am referring to the "soft" stages as they appear in Kegan's interpretation. Although I draw directly on the literature I have cited, I take full responsibility for my interpretation of the material. I believe that my reading conforms to the spirit of the most up–to–date and open version of American constructivist–developmental research. Since choices had to be made, my interpretation

---

[18]   E. H. Erikson, *Childhood and Society,* 2d ed., rev. and enl. (New York: W. W. Norton, 1963); *Identity: Youth and Crisis* (New York: W. W. Norton, 1968); *Insight and Responsibility. Lectures on the Ethical Implications of Psychoanalytic Insight* (New York: W. W. Norton, 1964).

[19]   See especially: W. G. Perry, Jr., *Forms of Intellectual and Ethical Development in the College Years: A Scheme* (New York: Holt, Rinehart and Winston, 1970); R. L. Selman, *The Growth of Interpersonal Understanding: Develomental and Clinical Analyses* (New York: Academic Press, 1980).

does not perfectly match that of any of the authors cited. This is particularly true of the two controversial stages of the postconventional level.

## Three Levels of Development

Whatever they call it, and however they describe it, the researchers we have referred to acknowledge the existence of a fundamental threefold movement in the way subjects situate themselves in relation to what is outside them, or in the way in which they make sense of the subject–object relationship. As Kegan has observed, the story of human development is the story of meaning–making.

At the first level of development the subjects, still embedded as they are in the concretely existential, do not escape from the tyranny of the actual and the singular. Their meaning–making is that of individuals in front of other concrete individuals whose decisions and personal initiatives have good or bad effects on them. Before what Piaget calls "formal operations" are in place, subjects do not have access to the world of abstraction. They have the ability to know and organize what actually exists, but not what might be. They have not acquired the skill needed to perceive reality as a category in a system. Psychosocially, it could not be otherwise. Even the notion of society as an abstract reality in which they hold membership escapes their understanding of human interactions.

Kohlberg termed "preconventional" this first level on which moral reason builds. This word aptly describes the type of relationships into which individuals, who have not yet built a conventional world, are capable of entering. Since they do not have, as it were, a membership card, they do not identify with social conventions. Even when interiorized by the mechanism Freud describes, these prohibitions remain "parental." The obligation does not arise from the rational self, but from the superego. Therefore, moral rules always seem irrelevant to moral subjects at the preconventional level.

The advancement to formal operations is the *sine qua non* of the passage to the totally other conventional moral universe, where the rules that we collectively agree upon are worked out. When the self emerges from the concreteness in which it has been stuck, it establishes mutual relationships with its fellows within the boundaries of a particular group. The interiorization of rules qualitatively changes their makeup. Rules are no longer promulgated by another's voice speaking within the self, but by "our collective voice." The subjects participate in a choir of voices. As individuals they appropriate the rules, not by a subconscious reconstruction, but through social identification. The rules of the group to which the individuals belong are also their very own, and oblige them inasmuch as they are members. The balance between subject and object takes on new meaning. The subject, now differentiated from the concrete, grasps the concept of an abstract social code, and learns to deal with it.

According to Piaget's genetic theory of knowledge, the construction of formal operations, which usually takes place between the ages of 11 or 12 to 14 or 15, brings the sequence of development to an end. When Kohlberg assigned the last stage of moral development to boys 15 or 16 years of age during his doctoral research, he was depending on Piaget's epistemology. But, when they were old enough for college, many of these youths began to think as they had at stage 2. In 1973, Kohlberg and his colleagues announced that they had erred in scoring the results. They stated that the adolescents had actually only reached the second moral level. The conventional morality of young people undergoes a crisis during a transitory period of their advanced adolescence, before it is reshaped at a third level called postconventional. They labelled this period of crisis "stage 4 1/2."[20]

As John Gibbs realized, the new interpretation of the postconventional level should logically lead to the abandonment of Piaget's concept of knowledge.[21] The crisis of conventional morality is not prompted by the attainment of a new level of logical competence. The new meaning–making is the product of critical reflection. The crisis is provoked by a meta–ethical questioning of the nature of these social rules which do not always turn out to be just or manage to give each member what is his or her due. This reflection prompts the subjects to take their distance from the social system with which they have totally identified, and in which they have felt warm and comfortable, and invites them to move towards a new level of differentiation where they stand as subjects before an objectified social system.

Postconventional moral discernments, consequently, can differ from those of the group. The subjects have gone beyond positive law to construct a notion of justice. Their

[20]   E. Turiel, "Conflict and Transition in Adolescent Moral Development," *Child Development,* Vol. 45, 1974, pp. 14–29.

[21]   J. C. Gibbs, "Kohlberg's Stages of Moral Judgment: A Corrective Critique," *Harvard Educational Review,* Vol. 47, 1977, pp. 43–61.

perspective is that of the moral exigencies anterior to a specific social situation.

As early as 1923, Piaget expressed one of his fundamental insights into the constitutional egocentricity of the infant's undifferentiated perspective, and the developmental tasks of "decentration."

> This attitude [the egocentricity of childish thought] consists in an absorption of the self in things and in the social group so that the subject thinks that he really knows things and people while, in reality, he adds qualities, which originate in his own self or in his particular perspective, to their objective qualities. . . . A subject emerges from his egocentricity, not by acquiring new knowledge about things or the social group, nor by turning towards the object as something exterior, but by decentralizing himself, and disassociating the subject from the object.[22]

Kohlberg's theory of the three levels of development brilliantly illustrates this insight. In Piaget's nomenclature, which interprets the movement towards moral development as a transition from heteronomy to autonomy, moral decentration is often understood in terms of a submission to, or an emancipation from, an exterior law. This interpretation leaves Kohlberg open to Edward Sullivan's complaint that his ideology is liberal and individualistic.[23] However, the idea of the subject's progressive liberation should not be understood as the transition from a social to an individual-

---

22    J. Piaget, *Le langage et la pensée de l'enfant* (Neuchâtel: Delachaux et Niestlé, 1923), pp. 69–70. The quotes in the text are translated from chapter 2, a chapter which has not been translated in *The Language and Thought of the Child* (New York: Meridian, 1955).

23    E. V. Sullivan, "A Study of Kohlberg's Structural Theory of Moral Development: A Critique of Liberal Social Science Ideology," *Human Development,* Vol. 20, 1977, pp. 352–376.

istic identity. The truth is more complex than that. To get a firmer grip on the nature of development, we must examine the bipolar movement that characterizes each level.

## Two "Psychologics" of Evolutionary Adaptation

Robert Kegan has given the most satisfactory explanation of the movement Kohlberg detected within each level and conveyed in the idea of the double series of stages. We falsify the sense of moral meaning–making if we simplify Kohlberg by dropping the important articulation of the three levels, and retain only the six stages.

To understand properly the constitutive movement of each level, we have to take vital adaptation, the fundamental insight of Piaget's genetic epistemology, seriously. The epistemological undertaking of Piaget originated in the reading he did into the origin of human thought, while still quite young. Rightly or wrongly, Piaget heard the philosophers he was reading giving two answers. One was idealist: ideas are preformed in the subject who imposes an intellectual order on the world. The other was environmentalist: the intelligible forms are in the physical world and gradually impose themselves on the subject's intellect. Piaget rejected the second. He thought that the interactions of the intellect with the surrounding world were what needed to be studied because all thought, even the most abstract, is an interiorized action, an "operation." Today this approach is labelled interactionist or constructivist.

Piaget began, therefore, to study scientifically infants' interaction with their environment. He concluded that every human function, including understanding which is the highest, is fundamentally an adaptation involving two movements: an assimilation which transforms the milieu (the object) so that the subject can integrate it into the self, and an accommodation which modifies the subject's plan of action to take into account those properties of the object which cannot be assimilated directly. Once assimilation and accommodation are in equilibrium, human behaviour is adapted. All adaptation, however, is provisional and dynamic because the object never stops revealing other aspects of itself to the subject. When confronted with new challenges, the subject does not destroy the acquired form of equilibrium. By a new accommodation, it reshapes it into a higher organization, that is, into a structure capable of a qualitatively superior assimilation.[24]

Kegan demonstrates his ingenuity by identifying the bipolar movement of each moral level of Piaget's adaptation.[25] He suggests conceiving the evolutionary activity as a helix oscillating between two psychologics at each level. One fosters inclusion, attachment, being–with and integration. This matches Piaget's assimilation. The other fosters independence, detachment, autonomy and differentiation. This matches Piaget's accommodation. In this way, the subjects gradually divest themselves of coercive elements by putting them back into the objective world from which they come. Development is a kind of hatching out of the subjects, their emergence from the world in which they have been embedded until then. It is a birth of the subjects to

---

[24]  H. Ginsburg and S. Opper, *Piaget's Theory of Intellectual Development: An Introduction* (Englewood Cliffs: Prentice–Hall, 1969), pp. 17-19.

[25]  R. Kegan, *The Evolving Self: Problem and Process in Human Development* , pp. 106–110.

themselves. When they get a grip on their own subjectivity, they also improve the quality of their operations with the more clearly defined object. "The psychological meaning of evolution," Kegan writes, is "a lifetime activity of differentiating and integrating what is taken as self and what is taken as other."[26]

Differentiation and integration are, then, consecutive responses to the complexity of the interaction of subjects with their world. Each movement leads to an "evolutionary truce" which is a state of equilibrium in the definition of the subject in regard to his or her dealings with the world. This equilibrium, however, is unstable since the tension is resolved at the first stage in favour of inclusion and, in the following, in favour of independence. Each truce involves not only the consolidation of gains, but also the reception of new, unfamiliar elements that initiate the next change.

We must not follow certain hasty, purely psychological interpretations of the sequence of development and imagine that subjects stand alone, struggling against an abstract and inert environment.[27] As far as the subjects are concerned, the environment is what Kegan calls *a culture of embeddedness.*[28] This is a psychosocial reality which is part of the self, but which also has its own, objective reality. Inasmuch as this amniotic environment is social, it fulfils three functions. First, it serves as an evolutionary host,

---

[26] *Ibid.,* p. 76.

[27] For an example see, A. Skolinck, *The Intimate Environment: Exploring Marriage and the Family* (Boston: Little, Brown, 1978), pp. 305–311.

[28] R. Kegan, *The Evolving Self: Problem and Process in Human Development*, pp. 113–116 and 121–132.

like the uterine wall to which the embryo attaches itself. Second, it must agree to let go of the subject trying to be born. Third, it must stay put to enable the detached subject to form a new relationship with what used to be part of him or herself. If understood in this way, the sequence of moral development is not based on an "individualistic ethic," with a social ethic artificially tacked on as an afterthought.

Moral development turns out to be an autotranscendence that frees the subject from all that hinders the reception of the other. By enlarging the range of the object and by projecting everything that is not the self in front of the self, the subject leaves room for the other to become authentically other. Moral development represents the successive triumphs of the relation to the other over embeddedness in a world that is not clearly differentiated from the self. The secret of moral development is the quality of the differentiation from the other; the more completely the subjects give birth to the self, the better the quality of their presence to the other and the world.

## Stages of Development and Ethical Models

If "morality" is taken in the existential sense of a set of rules of conduct, and "ethics" as the ordering of a set of rules of conduct, or reflection thereon, the authors mentioned have used the words correctly when they speak of moral development. They claim to describe the stages their subjects pass through in experiencing the set of rules that govern their conduct.

Throughout the centuries, however, philosophers and theologians have presupposed that everyone experiences the rules of conduct in the same way. They have reflected, accordingly, on the so–called common experience and explained how discernment and moral behaviour function. The reflection of these thinkers is really based, however, on the moral experience to which they have access. Is their ethics, then, anything more than the systematization of the point of view appropriate to their own stage of development?[29]

To appreciate the truth of this hypothesis, we have to note that all researchers admit that not all human beings complete the sequence of moral development in their lifetime; quite the contrary. Kohlberg has always maintained that less than a quarter of Americans reach the third level. Authors who want to describe the structure of stage 6 have to look for evidence in the biographies of historical figures renowned for their exceptional moral grandeur. Researchers who assign ages to each stage take care to mention that they are only indicating the threshold for the earliest passage from one stage to another.

François Grégoire writes that "a moral doctrine is nothing more than the ordered form taken by an almost sentimental *intuition* about the meaning or non–meaning of the universe and, therefore, of human existence, predating any philosophical construct."[30] Is that not exactly what a stage of moral development means for the researchers we have considered: a global reading of the ultimate meaning or

---

[29] L. Kohlberg himself has mentioned that the stages could be thought of as "separate moral philosophies": "The Child as a Moral Philosopher," *Psychology Today,* Vol. 2, Sept. 1968, p. 25.

[30] F. Grégoire, *Les grandes doctrines morales* (Paris: Presses Universitaires de France, 1967), p. 7.

non–meaning of existence, made within the human subject's experience ("intuition," *intus legere*)?

The six chapters which follow consider each stage as it emerges from the empirical research, and use historical examples to suggest the ethical model to which it corresponds. We must not forget that the experience of the adult and the experience of the child are not identical, even if both employ, for example, stage 2 reasoning. If, in addition, this adult is a philosopher, his or her sophistication will strip the model of its customary innocence.

## Relevance to Faith

The explanations of the stages and the corresponding ethical models will bring out both the intuitions that are acceptable, and the limitations that are characteristics of each model. Is that not, after all, the focus of this book? The question is what is at stake in the humanization of individuals and communities when they use a particular ethical model ?

If the quality of humanization is at stake in an ethical model, the same is true of the quality of faith. When they wonder about what is specifically Christian in ethics, theologians traditionally follow the trajectory of "deductive faith" which proceeds from pronouncements about God to interpretations of human experience.[31] They try to discover what revealed religion tells us about moral conduct in terms of moral precepts, privileged moral values and promises of interior help.

---

[31]   P. L. Berger, *A Rumor of Angels: Modern Society and the Recovery of the Supernatural* (New York: Anchor Books, 1975), pp. 71–72.

These are legitimate considerations. But, nowadays, theology spontaneously follows "inductive" faith, which starts from human experience and concludes with pronouncements about God. This faith is illustrated in Paul VI's statement to the Council Fathers: "To know God, we must know man."[32] Why? Because "no one has ever seen God" (John 1:18). In Christian tradition, as in all other religious traditions, the community receives a revelatory word about the divinity from privileged witnesses: "It is the only Son, who is nearest to the Father's heart, who has made him known" (John 1:18). "Father" is just a word. Whoever bears the title must invest it with meaning. The most radical aspect of faith is the cognitive and affective link that relates us to the divine reality through the evocation of a word such as "father." But the quality of this linkage depends, in large part, on the quality of the human experience which informs it.

The form of moral experience that each stage represents has a considerable impact on the choice and quality of the symbols each one uses to relate to God. Moral experience, as such, does not generate faith. But when faith is present, it does condition its human quality.

---

[32] *Documentation Catholique,* Vol. 63, 1966, p. 65.

# Chapter One

# Impulsive Stage
# and Hedonistic Ethics

## Pre–Moral Stage

Is there an initial period of life when the human being cannot be said to have a moral existence in any acceptable sense of the word? All researchers in the field of moral development think there is. Their sequences usually start with stage 0, which is the amoral or pre–moral stage of the first years of life. If little babies have no awareness of obligatory rules, it is because they have no sense of themselves as subjects. They are so embedded in their world that they do not hear even the faintest call to be better than they are.

"Sensorimotor" was the word Piaget used to describe infant intelligence. Embedded as it is in the world of sensible reflexes, this intelligence is activated solely by its physical surroundings. It functions without thought, abstract concepts or language. Infants, armed as they are with this purely practical, perceptual intelligence, which they quickly put into operation, function in their environment like a thing among the other things with which they come in contact. These things only become real for them when they can be experienced by the senses. If they are removed from the range of the senses, they cease to exist in the child's mental universe.

If we define the self as that which constitutes the individuality of a human being, we can only attribute this analogically to the central sensorimotor reflex of little babies. Although children are totally automatistic, the supporting culture does exercise control through the person who cares for their needs. In describing the oral phase of the first year of life, Freud said more about the warmth of the caregiver than about the nursing infant.[1] Babies get the feeling that the world is a good or bad place from the nurturing attitude of their immediate family. Consequently, they feel at ease or anxious, secure or insecure in their world. Freud's first sexual phase is a sensual experience of the kind of future the child can expect in his or her world. Erikson also describes the psychodynamic apprenticeship in terms of a basic trust versus a basic mistrust of life. The successful completion of this apprenticeship lays the foundation for the indispensable virtue of hope.[2]

---

[1]     S. Freud, "Three Essays on the Theory of Sexuality," *The Standard Edition* (London: Hogarth Press, 1953), Vol. 7, pp. 125–245, remains the classic reference for the sexual stages.

[2]     E. H. Erikson describes the apprenticeship tasks of the eight "ages of man" in *Childhood and Society,* 2nd ed. (New York: W.W. Norton, 1963), and in *Identity: Youth and Crisis* (New York: W. W. Norton, 1968). He elaborates the virtues characteristic of each age in *Insight and Responsibility: Lectures on the Ethical Implications of Psychoanalytic Insight* (New York: W.W. Norton, 1964), pp. 111–157.

There is no "other" in the inner life of young babies. Strictly speaking, they do not engage in social or moral interaction. When babies grasp fingers, look at people, smile and babble, they are deploying a remarkable range of skills in an effort to seduce the one caring for them and, in this way, to integrate themselves into their environment. An adult, who is sufficiently free from the tyranny of primary needs to be able to recognize these efforts to be attached, provides the warmth children need to be able to differentiate themselves eventually from the nourishing culture. For the moment, however, they are as enclosed in it as unhatched birds are within their shells.

Unfortunately, some human beings do not receive a warm response from an adult and spend a long period of time, sometimes their whole lives, in their shells. Until some generous and skilled people or professional counsellors free them from this prison, they live like shadows of themselves and remain radically incapable of responsible moral behaviour.

## The Impulsive Subject

When confronted with a problem, young babies do not start by reflecting on how to resolve it. They respond by actions which become more and more complex as the children evolve. Piaget describes their trajectory in his six stages of sensorimotor intelligence. At about two years of age the child begins to "think before acting." What has happened? The actions they have been performing from their birth for the sake of survival are interiorized by repetition. As this interiorization proceeds, things can disappear from the sensorial range of the children without vanishing from their mental universe. Children retain the remembered image and thus guarantee the permanence of the object. They can "hatch out" of the world that surrounds them, and take a distance from it that extends ever wider in space and time. Children now have a mental map of their little world. They have even started to decipher some of the elementary links of causality.

These mental feats represent a giant step forward in the process of adaptation. They indicate that children have gone beyond physicality, immediacy and the tangible. Historicity, distantiation and the symbolic have entered the picture. The world of the mental object has been born. Children set out to conquer it by constructing instruments as marvellous as deferred imitation, fantasy, drawings, dreams, play and, especially, language. Piaget says that the "collective monologues" of young children who use language are not a means of communication but a stimulant and mode of self–expression.[3]

Correlative to the constitution of the object by representation, perceiving subjects take shape. These subjects are no longer the victims of their reflexes but their co-ordinators. They have acquired the wonderful power of activating them, prolonging them, discontinuing them, directing them towards the object of their choice, imagining them, remembering them, speaking about them before, during and after they exercise them. At last they can express the sense of being themselves.

We must not, however, exaggerate the extent of the cultural revolution preschool children inaugurate. At this

---

[3]    J. Piaget, *The Language and Thought of the Child* (New York: Meridian Books, 1955); *Play, Dreams, and Imitation in Childhood* (New York: Norton, 1964).

stage their mental representations have not yet become abstract concepts. Piaget speaks of "preconcepts." These representations evoke only specific realities: "this dog," "that house," not "dog" or "house." At this stage children's thought is still too embedded in perceptions for the subjects to establish genres and classes of objects. Children cannot admit that two differently shaped containers into which the same amount of water has been poured, really are equal in volume. This frequently proven fact shows that children think on the basis of sensible appearance and do not use the kind of abstract operation that says that, since A = B and A = C, B = C. In the same way they do not distinguish another's point of view from their own. When they say "dog" or "house," they presume that their hearers have the same concrete images as they do. For the same reason they also confuse reality and fantasy.

Once they have mastered their reflexes, these neo–subjects must psychologically negotiate with this nascent autonomy. What an about–face this is in comparison with the blessed self–assurance of the previous stage! Will they exercise this new self–control without losing the self–esteem they have acquired? Will they, on the contrary, surrender the ground they have gained out of the shame they feel at being exposed to the other who might sneak up on them from "behind" (Freudian anality) ? Will they doubt their achievements because the external control exerted by another threatens their self–will? This is the drama Erikson, who follows Freud, describes when he evokes "autonomy" versus shame and doubt. Little children, who enter into the formidable "no" phase at about two years of age, proclaim to those around them that this evolutionary drama has begun. They are trying to structure wills fit for subjects.

A prudent culture of embeddedness acknowledges their self–affirmative efforts. It supports them in their first confrontation with existential anxiety, but it does not try to make these negative emotions disappear. They are part of the movement of a life which must free itself from the securities tying it down before it can take flight. An appropriate adult response is directed towards the anxious child rather than towards his or her anxiety. It helps the child to make sense of the grief felt at the loss of the old naively comfortable self. The child who is determined to continue life's journey must let go of that self.

Little people about two years of age are saying to themselves that they are individual beings. They have worked to guarantee their autonomy by keeping their rivals at arm's length. They have stood up on their own two legs and walked. By walking they have gone off on their own. They have not, then, been stationary. They can also be whatever they might wish to be. By assuming fantastic identities they can live extraordinary adventures in their imagination. Between three and five their playful selves set out to explore the world. These initiatives, however, create new problems that must be confronted. Leaving the beaten paths and stepping outside the old boundaries exposes them to guilt feelings.

Freud, who has given a sexual interpretation to this period, labels it the "phallic" phase. On the one hand, he describes the triangular sexual drama in which the children and their parents are engaged and, on the other, he evokes the genital games in which the young sensualists, eager for adventure, secretly indulge. But sexuality is only the most intimate aspect and the symbol of the whole existence of the child at this playful age. The danger these mini–prospectors run are many. The family, therefore, becomes the teacher drawing the line between the end of play and fantasy, and the beginning of reality. In doing this the family resembles the *paidagôgos* of antiquity, brandishing the rod.

The denial of the right to crawl into the conjugal bed is only the most impressive of all parental interdictions. Sensual "explorations" are limited on all sides: their bodies cannot be exposed in public; the electrical appliances can be used only by adults; the walls must not be smeared with paint; they only have access to the cookie jar and other goodies according to a tightly restricted schedule. The emergence of the permitted and the forbidden causes a split in the ego. From now on it has a childish, exuberant, imaginative element and a parental, self–observant, self–punishing element. The ego has built the superego, its in–house censor.

Once they have managed to explore the world within certain limits, without losing their curiosity and taste for adventure, preschool children acquire what the Erikson school calls the virtue of purpose. Purposeful people do not sink under the weight of guilt. They continue to be imaginative, effervescent and enterprising. In Fowler's terminology, this is the intuitive–projective phase and, in Kegan's, the impulsive.

## Moral Heteronomy

To make sense of the moral portrait of the young child it should be painted on the canvas of the cognitive, psychological and social structures considered above. When he examined the way that his young subjects interpreted moral dilemmas, Kohlberg decided to retain the term "heteronomy" that Piaget had applied to the initial moral stage. To distinguish clearly his first stage from the following, he added the words "punishment and obedience." According to Kohlberg, these terms show how young children understand morality, namely, that they identify moral good with the very act of obedience and evil with punishment. Kohlberg, obviously, elaborates this. However, because of the limitations of his research tools, he was never able to paint a picture of childhood morality as startling as we find in *The Moral Judgment of the Child.* Piaget's most lasting contribution relates to the moral experience of children at the heteronomous stage.

The way the young Genevans understood the origin of the rules for a game of marbles, moral rules or even lying shows that, in their eyes, every rule comes from adults and is invested with a sacred and intangible character. The morality of childhood is theocratic and gerontocratic. Children do not sit on the council of the gods and elders where the fate of humanity is decided. They have no say in the matter. Their role is to obey.

If we stick with these affirmations, however, we falsify the reality of their moral experience. Their "obedience" is less confining than the children's statements about it suggest. In line with the way children make sense of reality, moral obligation is something alien, something "out there." Their conduct is neither enlightened nor profoundly transformed by the obligations they accept uncomprehendingly. The young children solemnly told Piaget that no rule established by "grown–ups" could be changed. Nonetheless, when playing, they paid no attention to many rules of the game, wrongly interpreted those they had learned and, to all intents and purposes, played as they liked.

The study on lying produced similar results. Young children do not distinguish between swear words, obscenities and lies. Only the fact that they are forbidden makes them "naughty words." Children do not attribute the evil of lying to the liar's intent to deceive. It comes solely from adult censure. In this childish logic it follows that an unbelievable lie, ill–suited to fool grown–ups, is naughtier than another because it is more likely to be censured. Young children, generally, think that it is naughtier to say that they have seen a dog as big as a cow than to deny that they have been squabbling.

Since obligation is something external, it is also a purely material thing. It means conforming their conduct to the physical order of the world in which they are evolving. The greater the disaster one causes, whether willingly or unwillingly, the greater the ill will. Breaking fifteen cups completely by accident is fifteen times as naughty as breaking one while violating a parental rule. Consequently, the bigger the punishment, the greater the crime. Punishment is vindictive. It re-establishes the material order of the world that the fault has disrupted. There are no grey areas in the "moral" world of children. Grey areas come from thinking about degrees of intentionality. Here, however, since they are material and exterior, good and evil can be thought of as clearly measurable quantities. Separating the rye from the wheat is not an insoluble problem for them.

In accord with the exteriority and materiality of the obligation, responsibility is taken literally in this childhood morality. There is no such thing as "the spirit of the law" where the subjects have no access to the meaning–making of the legislator. Responsibility means essentially not getting caught with their mouth full of chocolate before meals, not getting caught walking on a freshly waxed floor with muddy sneakers, not fiddling in their pockets in front of strangers. If you're not caught, you're not guilty! The law has a purely penal character. Basically, it punishes the clumsiness of those who don't know how to manage. Wickedness is equivalent to a lack of know–how. When children are asked about the punishments appropriate to various infractions they usually do not choose a punishment that is meant to teach a lesson. They opt for the punishment that, by its severity, is most dissuasive and expiatory.

Although children from six to seven years of age know how to submit themselves to an absolute norm, they do not abandon overnight the quest for pleasure that characterizes the pre–moral stage. Despite the austere sound of "heteronomous stage: punishment/obedience," in children's eyes the human good remains the exercise of pleasure. After the differentiation of the first stage, which gives them an assured control of their sensorimotor reflexes, they begin to discern which family rules guarantee a happier life and which stand in their way. If children value obedience, it is as a means of increasing the coefficient of pleasure, not as an end in itself. Neither Piaget's experiments nor Kohlberg's moral protocols show us children enamoured of obedience for its own sake. It always appears as a necessary manoeuvre to avoid the ultimate evil: divine–parental retribution. Practising obedience out of love of obedience presupposes a subject's detachment from self. This is incompatible with the structural egocentrism of children for whom points of view, other than their own, do not exist.

## Childish Morality?

The major consequence of this description of the heteronomy of the first moral stage is that we can hear correctly what children are saying about good and evil. Once we have heard them, we can accurately interpret their behaviour. Interpreting their deeds and acts, according to a meaning–making to which they have no access, demonstrates a lack of respect for their personal integrity.

Should we even use the word "moral" when speaking about them? The current literature on the initiation into a moral universe tends to reserve the adjective "moral" for the activities of a postconventional elite because a "fundamental option" and heteronomy cannot be reconciled.[4] The research on moral development forces us to nuance the rigidly univocal conception of moral existence underlying the theory of the fundamental option. Once subjects become conscious of the normative rules of conduct, they enter into the area of morality. Children endowed with a superego can no longer avoid having their actions confronted by its censure. By judging their duties and behaviour according to a law that is not of their own making, children serve an indispensable apprenticeship in the moral discernments handed on by the culture in which they are embedded. Their success in learning and applying the rules of family behaviour contribute to their survival and to the establishment of a rudimentary moral know–how. They cannot, however, be held responsible for the moral quality of the rules they

---

[4] J. Fuchs, *Human Values and Christian Morality* (London: Gill & Macmillan, 1970), pp. 92–111; B. Häring, *Free and Faithful in Christ: Moral Theology for Clergy and Laity,* Vol. I (New York: Seabury Press, 1978), pp. 164–208.

apply because these rules originate in the moral discernment of their parents. If they regard masturbating as
"naughty," not only when it is done in public, but when it
is done in private, this is because someone else thinks so.
In this sense they are "moral" or "immoral" only by proxy.

Therefore, as far as the content of the rules applied to
conduct is concerned, current reservations about attributing
a "moral" existence to children are justified. They are also
pertinent when it comes to interpreting the meaning and the
consequences of the good and evil acts of children.

As far as meaning is concerned, adults should understand that what adults generally consider bad may be seen
quite differently by normal children. For children, successfully using words or acts to hide something adults forbid is
good, while moral adults think this behaviour wrong. Who
is right? Both are, according to their respective way of
making sense of human interactions. Children, who do not
learn to use deception to make their way in a world where
big people hold all the power, will not fulfil the cognitive,
psychological and social tasks that are essential for their
survival. Bruno Bettelheim has brilliantly shown that this
is precisely the lesson that popular, traditional wisdom
drills into children through fairy tales. It teaches them that,
in the land of giants, only the astute survive.[5] Labelling this
comparison of what a lie means for adults and for children
"subjectivist" does not shed any light on the issue. The
moral object that subjects construct is the only objectivity
that exists, as far as they are concerned. This is the frame-

---

[5]    B. Bettelheim, *The Uses of Enchantment: The Meaning and Importance of Fairy Tales* (New York: Knopf, 1976).

work within which they must learn to humanize their conduct.

This realization does not eliminate the responsibility that adults have to help children gradually acquire a more adequate sense of truthfulness. The impulsive stage is an evolutionary truce that calls for the integration of moral perceptions of a higher quality. It is just as erroneous to attribute a tragic dimension to children's deceptions and tricks. When Vladimir Jankélévitch, to whom we are indebted for his penetrating analysis of truthfulness, speaks of childish deceptions as "the first crease on the smooth face of innocence" and "the first shadow to darken the spotless linen of our guilelessness," he demonstrates his failure to understand the evolutionary role of these childish actions by interpreting them in terms of an adult scenario of duplicity.[6]

A correct interpretation of children's morality is also important to measure properly the significance of the good or bad actions they perform. The less they have given birth to the self, the less able they are to commit themselves fully to the path of good or the path of evil. Children who are still centred on a strictly unilateral perspective are incapable of actions that are of cosmic proportions. In fact, since they are radically incapable of adopting someone else's point of view, we cannot even speak of human reciprocity in their regard. This does not stop them from causing material disasters! Young children have set major fires and caused the loss of human lives. But they do not fully commit themselves, in the usual sense of the term, even in

---

[6]    V. Jankélévitch, *Traité des vertus* (Paris: Bordas, 1968–1972), Vol. 2, p. 457.

these materially destructive acts because they do not differentiate the world of intentionality from the exterior, material world. Since a considered decision is lacking, the good
or bad actions of children do not carry an eternal weight.
Their works are not the masterpieces of the accomplished
artist, but the daubings or copies of an apprentice. If we
judge the latter as though they are the former, we misunder-
stand them, and treat their creators unjustly.

## Stage One Adults?

James Fowler tells us that, when he was a teenager, he
worked one summer as a garbageman. One day, he and
Pete, the truck driver, began to discuss the speed of a white
Chevrolet in front of them. Pete would not admit that this
vehicle was travelling at the same speed as his truck because, as he insisted, it was not behind them but in front of
them.[7] If similar patterns of argument confirmed his use of
this type of logic, we would have to conclude that Pete is
an adult who has not gone beyond the pre–operational stage
of thought characteristic of preschool children. Since the
acquisition of concrete operational thought is a necessary,
though not sufficient, condition to progress beyond the first
stage of moral development, in all likelihood Pete's moral
judgments take the form of those of children of five or six
years of age.

Other adults may have acquired operational thought
without successfully handling the fundamental psychodynamic tasks of childhood. Equipped as they are with a self
without hope, will or purpose; gnawed by suspicion,

---

[7]     J. Fowler, "Life/Faith Patterns," in J. Berryman (ed.), *Life Maps*
(Waco: Winston Press, 1978), p. 15 and p. 25.

shame, doubt and guilt; their chances of taking a moral step beyond the heteronomy of a castrating superego are slim.

Usually very young children provide the protocols that illustrate the impulsive stage. Some protocols, however, record the views of older children and even of adolescents and adults. The moral protocols of adults still operating at the most elementary moral level may prove harder to score. Conjugal, parental, professional and other tasks have enriched their life experience, and given their words and gestures connotations not found in the sampling of young children. Nonetheless, basically the moral vision is the same. The only difference is likely to be the adult components of language and experience.

We are more likely to let ourselves be lured by a philosopher's discourse. The scholar will rarely display a logic as underdeveloped as that which Pete, the garbageman, used. However, moral discernment cannot be reduced to a logical thought process. It relies on other human factors that philosophers and moral theologians can lack. It would be quite surprising if we did not find among them individuals who have ethical characteristics corresponding to the first stage of moral development. All the philosophers and theologians who wholly or partly use this model are not necessarily stuck at the impulsive stage. The interpretations they give may modify the significance of this. It remains true, nonetheless, that the basic positions of this model depict an adult moral philosophy, the potential of which for human development does not go beyond the possibilities of the impulsive stage. This model is called hedonism.

## The Hedonist Model

Hedonism, from the Greek word *hedonê* (pleasure, delight, pleasantness, satisfaction), is a doctrine that makes the quest for pleasure the principle guiding the organization of morality. In western tradition, the Greek philosopher, Epicurus (341–270), stands as the leader of this ethical school which identifies pleasure as the sovereign good.[8] All the specialists agree that Epicurus' philosophy did not stupidly extol the quest for gross pleasures. Their agreement, however, ends there. An interpreter such as Karl Jaspers sees the father of Epicureanism as a hedonistic egotist and a consummate individualist.[9] Epicurus would, then, have had a stage one vision of morality. Others, however, see Epicurus as an altruistic hedonist who, as a real precursor of Jesus, preached and practised brotherly love. This is the interpretation, for example, of Norman De Witt.[10] According to this interpretation, the Epicureanism of Epicurus would not be the hedonism we are discussing in this text.

The key position of hedonism is the identification of the good with pleasure and evil with pain. Pleasure is the first and last word on "the good life." When we have pleasure, we've got it all; we are fulfilled. When it is absent, we have to do all we can to get it back. The first moral imper-

---

[8] On the thought of Epicurus, see W. Riley, *Men and Morals: The Story of Ethics* (New York: F. Ungar, 1960), pp. 152–162; C. Bailey, *The Greek Atomists and Epicurus: A Study* (Oxford: Clarendon Press, 1928), pp. 217–523.

[9] K. Jaspers, *Die grossen Philosophen* (München: R. Piper, 1981), Vol. 1, pp. 78–114.

[10] N. De Witt, *Epicurus and His Philosophy* (Minneapolis: University of Minnesota Press, 1954).

ative is clear: "Do whatever gives pleasure and avoid whatever causes pain."

On the basis of the physics of Democritus, Epicurus thought that pleasure was innate to human nature and that, if we surrender ourselves to our natural inclinations, they will give us pleasure. Epicurus, however, had enough experience and practical wisdom to know that debauchery would not deliver the pleasure so fervently desired. Consequently, he taught the need to practise discernment in responding to the psycho–physiological stimuli of our nature.

According to Epicurus, all pleasure is not desirable nor is all pain necessarily to be shunned. We should seek out pleasure, if it is only pleasure. We should flee from it, if it brings greater suffering. We should avoid suffering when it is only suffering. We should accept it, if it eventually yields a greater satisfaction. Thus the really moral person ought to practise a calculating prudence. Normative hedonistic ethics comes down to, or just about comes down to, a wise hierarchization of pleasures and pains. For Epicurus, the most perfect pleasures are *ataraxia,* liberation from mental agitation; *phronêsis,* wisdom; and *philia,* friendship with a restricted number of close acquaintances.

For a philosopher like Epicurus, the hedonist ideal is to live a balanced life that is frugal and obscure while envying no one so as not to be unhappy, harming no one so that reprisals are avoided, and combatting bearable pain by skilfully recalling happy memories. The sage, however, will know when to put an end to an intolerable life by suicide. Without pleasure, human life has no *raison d'être.*

This ethical model spans the ages. An anglicized Christian version is found in the work of Thomas Hobbes

(1588–1679).[11] Using a materialist and sensualist philo-sophical anthropology as his base, he developed the concept that has been labelled "ethical egotism." Good and evil are the equivalents of the pleasure and pain each indi-vidual experiences. It is natural for every individual to seek nothing more than his or her preservation and pleasure. Na-ture, then, is a state of war of all against all *(bellum omnium contra omnes)*. This disastrous situation is avoided by the intervention of *Leviathan*, the all–powerful state, which es-tablishes an equilibrium among the competing appetites by force. We also find in Hobbes a theological sanction theory in which the will of God is the source of natural law just as the state is the source of positive law. This vision of good and evil and of how the authority of "grown–ups" functions is not substantially different, all in all, from what children at the impulsive stage might construct at their own level.

## Role of Pleasure

The positive value of the hedonist model is that it points out the role pleasure plays in our common quest for humanization and happiness. A secular spiritualistic ten-dency, which is often inspired by religion, would like us to deny our original sensual experience of incorporation. It despises corporality, one of the constituent aspects of hu-manity, and, therefore, the body's sensitivity and sensuali-ty. In every age, right from the time of the apostles, the Church has had to distance itself from the dualistic currents that tend to demean physical reality. The Church has done

---

[11]   On the thought of T. Hobbes, see W. Riley, *Men and Morals: The Story of Ethics,* pp. 229–241; D. D. Raphael, *Hobbes: Morals and Poli-tics* (London: G. Allen and Unwin, 1978).

this because of its faith in the Incarnation and the Resurrection.

The hedonist model reminds us that sound, moderate and graded pleasures are signs that the actions of a creature, privileged to be an incarnate spirit, have met with success. Spurning pleasure is equivalent to despising the human creature God modelled from the earth, and into whose nostrils he breathed the breath of life (Genesis 2:7). The extreme dolorism that feeds the spiritualistic notion of humanity is a moral aberration. Though pain is part of human growth it, like pleasure, must never be sought for its own sake. Any ethical model that does not find a place for pleasure and pain betrays the integrity of the human experience. Hedonism's reflection on human pleasure makes a contribution to ethics.

## Egotistical Materialism

It should come as no surprise that Karl Marx, the father of contemporary dialectical materialism, began his philosophical career with a study of the philosophy of nature in the writings of Democritus and Epicurus.[12] The hedonistic ethical model is, in fact, built on a materialistic interpretation of human nature. Even a concept of pleasure that has room for friendship, peace and wisdom cannot free this position from the obsessive materialism of the anthropology underlying it. If individuals are logical about this, they primarily seek the satisfaction of their material needs, that is, sensorimotor needs that are quantifiable and measurable.

---

[12] K. Marx, "Über die Differenz der Demokritischen und Epikureischen Naturphilosophie," in H. J. Lieber and P. Furth (eds.), *Frühe Schriften* (Stuttgart: Cotta, 1962), Vol. 1, pp. 18–106.

Unless it betrays itself, this fundamental materialism cannot serve as the basis for an ethics that lifts individuals out of their infantile egotism. Sympathy may prompt hedonists to want a friend to have the same pleasure they desire, and they may find that this increases their own pleasure. But extending the pleasurable experience to another does not really involve a substantial decentralization. Sensory delight is felt only in the organism that produces it. The coincidence of a number of satisfying orgasms represents, at best, an increase in the volume of pleasure. The layer of agreeable sensory experience does not get qualitatively thicker because of the number who bed down in it. Savouring the abatement of sensory desire is, by its very nature, something individual and solitary. Any qualitative variation is the Spirit's work. By introducing elements like this, hedonism would exceed its own premises.

Even in its best versions, the hedonist ethic subjects individuals to a mechanistic natural order that presses down on them. No biological interpretation of the natural law is able to imagine subjects who are free. Individuals always look like they have been squeezed into prison garb. Their nature imposes a tyranny of needs on them: they have to eat, defecate, reproduce, relax, attack, retreat, etc. The confrontation of needs and desires brings individuals up against an impenetrable and alienating law: their own needs and desires are in conflict with the needs and desires of others. Regardless of their age, hedonists must perfect a system of peaceful coexistence with others and learn to please (obedience) and to hide the satisfaction of their needs and desires (avoidance of punishment), just as the heteronomous child at the impulsive stage does.

## Pietism and the God Who Rewards

The fact that no officially recognized moral theology claims the title "Christian hedonism" for itself does not mean that Christians and their pastors cannot live out a moral experience tailored to hedonism. This ethic is even more effective and uncontested when it hides behind pious phrases. If we had to call up historical examples, we could certainly point to Lutheran pietism at the beginning of this century, and to the pietism of certain contemporary American evangelical churches. All churches, however, shelter a more or less important and influential contingent of "pietists."

*Pietas* was traditionally thought of as an act and an attitude by which we pay homage to that which functions as a first principle in our lives. Filial piety is its prototype, piety towards God (such as, for example, Jesus showed towards his Father), the archetype. Piety is the consequence of a feeling of personal dependency of the kind a son or daughter has towards a parent.

Historically, the term "pietism" has been applied to any religious movement that reduces faith to a moral feeling of individual piety towards the Divine. In pietist movements the sources of revelation are less inspired than inspiring. They serve primarily to foster "good feelings" and emotions in the faithful. They quiet their anguish, console them in their disappointments, and encourage them to live virtuously because the just person "will live in prosperity, his children have the land for their own" (Psalm 25:13). Pious feelings also quiet their anger for "the arms of the wicked will be broken" (Psalm 37:17): thieves will be caught, hitmen will be punished, homosexuals and drug addicts will die of AIDS.

The religion and ethics pietists live by give those who mind their own business, and organize a moderate hierarchy of pleasures in their lives, an untroubled conscience. "Illegal" and shameful pleasures are at the bottom of the scale because, if their participation in these pleasurable activities were made public, there is too great a risk that a disproportionate displeasure would be provoked. On the other hand, safe pleasures, such as the legal acquisition of material wealth, bring social satisfactions and have, therefore, divine approval. Recently, when some multimillionaire American television evangelists were accused of sexual scandals, their colleagues and followers condemned their sexual misbehaviour and the shameful use to which, on these occasions, they had put their wealth. Few of them, however, cast any doubt on the legitimacy of the enormous monetary gains that came to them from their ministry. During a televised debate on an American network, one of their colleagues laid out the classic position of religious pietism. People should be paid, he said, according to their moral value and the moral services they render to the community. But ministers teach good morals and the police enforce them. In a well-ordered society ministers of religion and police officers should be the best paid.

The hedonistic way of life, and the doctrine of moral existence underlying religious pietism, decisively determines the attitudes taken towards God. As Christians, these hedonists can recite all the divine names found in the Bible, from the Yahweh Sabbaoth (God of the armies) of the oldest traditions to the God of Love of the Johannine writings. Nonetheless, over and above all these titles, the image of

God that effectively touches the living faith is conditioned by how believers make human sense of good and evil.

The hedonistic mode of meaning–making disposes the subject to relate to a Santa Claus God who leads his faithful children towards a land where milk and honey flow, a land of material superabundance. Towards evildoers, however, this God shows the face of a fierce ogre who takes pleasure in sadistically torturing troublemakers. Satanic imagery is never far from this perverse notion of a dual God: the God of reward and the God of punishment.[13] Is the God of Judaeo–Christian revelation essentially a God who dispenses rewards and punishments? Max Weber has brilliantly shown that, silhouetted behind "God Save America," is a God produced by the Protestant pietistic ethic that gave birth to the spirit of capitalism.[14]

---

[13]    M. Bellet, *Le Dieu pervers* (Paris: Desclée de Brouwer, 1979), and A.–M. Rizzuto, *The Birth of the Living God: A Psychoanalytic Study* (Chicago: The University of Chicago Press, 1979), pp. 18–22 and 41–53, show that the image of God is fashioned towards the end of the Oedipal period from an exultation of the objectified parents, and their subsequent division into God and Demon.

[14]    M. Weber, *The Protestant Ethic and the Spirit of Capitalism* (New York: Charles Scribner's Sons, 1958).

Chapter Two

# Imperial Stage
# and Utilitarian Ethics

## On the Way to Independence

At school age, between five and seven, children get ready to leave the impulsive stage. Robert Kegan recounts a delightful anecdote to illustrate this transition.

Late one afternoon, an eight-year-old boy decided that he was fed up with his family and announced to his parents that he was leaving home. His parents sympathetically helped him get ready to leave. While they packed various things into a grip, they said that they were going to miss him. They bid him goodbye, and the boy left the house. His parents watched his progress from the front window. A little way from the house the youngster met some of his friends who were playing. He put his bag down and joined in. When dinnertime came, all the children went home. The young fugitive stood still for a long time by himself.

Finally, he picked up his suitcase and dejectedly started to walk slowly towards the house.

His parents were apprehensive. Wouldn't this aborted effort to run away have negative consequences? When he came in, the little boy found his parents seated and ready to listen to him. He sat down in front of them, absorbed in his own thoughts. Not a word. Then, after a long minute, the cat burst into the living room. The boy looked up and said, "I see you still have that old cat!"[1]

His effort to run away may have failed but not his evolutionary journey. His return home signaled to his parents that he was coming back from a long trip that he had set off on two or three years earlier in order to tear himself away from the family culture in which his self was embedded. He did not come back to the house as a little child that you have to watch every second. As the father in the parable of the prodigal son (Luke 15:11–32) knew very well, the successful return of a son presupposes that he is welcomed in his dignity as son. The parents of our hero no longer have before them a little sensualist, totally absorbed in impulsive tasks. They are looking at a new self who has become aware of his role as son in the family structure, and of the independence that the role confers. They are his parents; he owes them obedience, but no longer is he their "thing." He is an individual, their son. He takes full possession of his filial privileges. An imperial self sits enthroned in that chair. What has happened in the life of this eight-year-old youngster to allow him to speak in such a detached way of "his parents' cat"? What new conquests must he prepare

---

[1]   R. Kegan, *The Evolving Self* (Cambridge: Harvard University Press, 1982), pp. 159–160.

for, now that he has returned home to assume his rightful place?

## Instrument for Conquest: Concrete Operation

Children of seven or eight years of age construct an amazing logic to conquer their world. Their thought has taken a quantum leap. Piaget labels this intelligence "concrete operational." An operation, in Piaget's use of the word, is an interiorized action with two characteristics. First, it is reversible. Reversibility means that a subject's effective action, classifying something, for example, or a change seen in the physical world such as, for example, the transformation of a ball of plasticine into a cylinder, can be cancelled in thought by an action in the inverse sense. Addition, then, is an operation because it can be reversed by subtraction. In the same way, the transformation of a lump of plasticine from form A to form B can be cancelled out by returning to form A. The second characteristic of an operation, according to Piaget, is its co-ordination into an operational structure. This means that the interiorized action represents a system that has its own laws, and that functions in the same way in relation to a plurality of contents.

This acquisition gives children a mobility of thought and a means to analyse the world's realities that they lacked when their thought was glued to perception. However, the evolutionary scope of the operational cognition should not be exaggerated. Piaget has marked its limits by labelling it "concrete." The operations of children from seven or eight to 11 or 12 years of age are directed solely towards the concrete. Classifications, seriations and ordinations are applied only to physical realities. The meaning–making of children is confined to what is real.

Concerned as they are to describe the concrete operations to which older children advance and the order in which they appear, Piagetian researchers are very like experts in logic; in fact, they are more like experts in logic than like specialists in child psychology. American researchers have often been better at seeing the psychodynamic implications of this new ability to think logically. Kegan, in particular, observes that the people around them are part of the concrete reality children can classify. They classify them, first of all, as "subjects" distinct from the category of "objects." Then, from among these, they distinguish the category of those who are "like them" (small, weak, English–speaking, students, girls, children) and those who are not (grown–ups, strong, French–speaking, teachers, boys, parents). These categories of subjects are arranged, classified, placed in a descending or ascending order, added to, subtracted from and so forth.

Through these operations, children construct the role that they and others play. They acquire a more exact concept of the self. These small individuals now know who they are in relation to the different categories in which they classify other people. They also begin to think of others as distinct from themselves, and benefit from points of view other than their own. The Oedipal crisis that began between three and five years of age can now be resolved. Children do not give up the *ménage à trois* scenario just because they know they are excluded from the conjugal bed. They only look for relationships elsewhere when they realize that they are excluded from family life for a certain period of time each day. The culture of embeddedness widens to include two new institutions, the school and peer culture.

If the school, peer group and the family, reconstituted according to the new roles, are part of a common psychosocial environment, it is because they all can support children in the organization of their roles so that they can distance themselves from their impulses and master them. At home, their parents tactfully allow them to play their roles as sons or daughters. Parents do this by their actions and their attitudes, such as showing an increased respect for children's privacy, letting them decorate their own rooms, giving them watches so they can manage "their time," and providing a weekly allowance. At school, children play their particular role in a more complex world where they must take their place while measuring themselves against the competition and the rules. In their peer group, children participate in a set of secular rituals of play and negotiations, the main point of which is to allow them to practise their role of being subjects. Participating in this last institution marks another first in the history of the evolution of the self. For the first time they actively share in organizing the culture in which they are embedded.

## Towards the Conquest of the World

It is not just because children construct their roles that Kegan calls the balance achieved around 10 or 11 the "imperial" stage. Actually, from the thrones where they sit as subjects, they acquire a whole new perspective on their kingdoms. They enter into a whole new relationship with the object. The world has become something that can be deciphered, organized and controlled. No longer is it the shifting thing it once was. These impulsive individuals used to be embedded in their impulses. The new terrain of their imperial selves is the concreteness of the world. Each of them proclaims to his or her family circle: "I am my concrete needs."

What a fascinating kingdom this concrete world is for children! Monarchs of their environment, they take stock of its data, its statistical laws and the exceptions to them, and its wonders. They try to figure out how the great physical machine works, and how to control it by the exact calculation of what it is going to do. These little individual selves acquire a new sense of their own agency and of the managerial skill they exercise for their own good. They develop a sharp awareness of the influence they have on what happens around them. They pass from being passive receivers to being active agents. The second stage, which objectifies impulses provides, then, a theory of impulses. These no longer possess the self, the self possesses them, and children organize them to serve their needs, desires and interests. Older children "wheel and deal" on their own. You see them whipping by on their bikes, expertly controlling the speed, busy, waving, shouting orders to God knows who, checking their big, black, digital wristwatches. They are obsessed with collecting all sorts of junk to cram into their pockets: picture cards of sports heroes, badges, comic strips and coins. They are always on the lookout for a chance to get one up on their competitors.

Erikson insightfully describes the considerable industry that is typical of this period. The shift in the interests of children in this stage, from affects to the "mechanical world," justifies Freud's description of this as "the latency period" of life. However, latency can no longer be understood to mean a time when sexual interests lie dormant. Carlfred Broderick has so convincingly documented that older children experience a variety of sexual activities and attitudes that it is no longer possible to sustain this idea.[2] It is true, nonetheless, that the dominant investment is no longer as sensual as it was during the psychologics of inclusion of early childhood. Assimilation through the balancing of impulses has given way to integration through work well done. Older children strive to gain recognition through what they make. They try to adjust themselves to the technological world.

Even in the sexual domain, the acquisition of knowledge about the "equipment" prevails over the other aspects of the sexual experience. Adults, who use the pretext of a lack of interest during the latency period to hold back information from children who have the right to it, produce results that are the opposite to what they intend. Children who are insufficiently informed sexually (in this day and age very few are totally uninformed) are more likely to experiment in an attempt to obtain knowledge than those who have been given explicit, precise and complete sexual information. All contemporary surveys support this.[3] Here, as in other areas, children owe it to themselves to develop what Erikson calls "the virtue of competence," that is, the ability freely to exercise their dexterity and intelligence in accomplishing the tasks that fall within the range of their capabilities. Blocking their access to sexual or other kinds

---

[2]   H. J. Ruppel, Jr., "Socio–sexual Development among Preadolescents," in J.–M. Samson (ed.), *Childhood and Sexuality* (Montreal and Paris: Éditions Études Vivantes, 1980), pp. 128–135.

[3]   M. Zelnik and Y. Kim, "Sex Education and its Association with Teenage Sexual Activity, Pregnancy, and Contraceptive Use," *Family Planning Perspectives,* Vol. 14, 1982, pp. 117–126; G. Moran, *No Ladder to the Sky: Education and Morality* (San Francisco: Harper & Row, 1987).

of information violates one of their most fundamental human rights.

Parents and teachers are used to seeing girls and boys who have been successful in the last stage of childhood pass through an evolutionary truce, during which they rule over a peaceful and ordered kingdom. When the adaptive balance shifts towards independence, in fact, subjects always display a high degree of self–assurance. The serene confidence produced by their sense of competence should not, however, be allowed to mask the weakness of the imperial self. There is certainly weakness in those selves who fail to acquire the level of competency necessary to survive with dignity, that is, who do not match their peers' capacity to order their world, to take it apart and put it together, to control it instead of being at its mercy. When their equipment fails, children generally develop an inferiority complex that can handicap them for life.

Even when the imperial self succeeds, its regime is more fragile than it appears. There is a price to be paid for attaining a new degree of independence. The price is loneliness. By its very nature, the competition that "energizes" school children prevents the creation of intimate bonds with others. Consequently, the imperial self, evolving in a world of its own, harbours a certain suspicion of others. Since imperial selves see others in terms of their own survival needs, they often manipulate them for their own ends. In this regard, they are troubled less by a sense of guilt than by their worry about how others are going to react. This uncomfortable situation, with its loneliness and worry, is a psychological factor pushing them towards the fusional stage.

## Moral Instrumentalism

The children we have just described do not know who their peers think they are. Trying to get an answer to the question of their intimate identity monopolizes the efforts of adolescents. What young people at the imperial stage know is what they are for themselves. They are concrete operators who are concerned about the success of what they do. They are completely absorbed in predicting the consequences of their acts, and the acts of the different groups of people who can easily break into their world. They no longer see themselves, as they did in the preschool period, as passive receivers of parental prohibitions, and of the rewards and punishments that fatefully follow their actions. They acquire a rather admirable level of skill in anticipating the reactions of those in authority and of their own peers. In the order of good and evil, this skill gives them the advantage of knowing how to manipulate the various actors who play a role in their daily lives. They know how to coax, amuse, soothe, outsmart and even how to bribe and blackmail. If they are in the ring and feel cornered, they know how to point the family's investigation towards their little sister. If, on the contrary, they come to the aid of their brother, who is about to be caught, they expect him to return the favour when they get into trouble.

Individuals at stage 2 always answer Kohlberg's moral dilemmas according to the logic of the law of the talon: "an eye for an eye, a tooth for a tooth." The negative formulation of the Golden Rule as it is found, for example, in the Book of Tobit (4:15) fits this minimalist interpretation perfectly: "Never do to another what you don't want that person to do to you." Kohlberg loves to cite the familiar expression, "Scratch my back, I'll scratch yours" to characterize stage 2 morality. This is the basic barter system of products and favours: *do ut des* (I'll swap you this for that). Kohlberg labels stage 2, the stage of mercantile morality, "instrumentalist." In this world of commercialized human relationships, a common, shared reality does not yet exist. Older children certainly count both girls and boys among their friends, but these friendships are essentially for mutual service and the exchange of reciprocal pleasures.

In instrumental morality, mutuality functions according to self–interest. Robert Selman, who has made a systematic study of the development of the bonds of friendship, shows that children at stage 2 do not think of friendship as a matter of interests shared but as something meant to serve the many particular concerns of the partners. Among the examples given, the following answer from a girl illustrates this instrumental understanding of friendship very well: "We are friends because she likes me and I like her too. We do things for one another." At stage 1 favours went only one way. A little girl at the impulsive stage stated : "She is not my friend anymore because she wouldn't come with me when I wanted her to."[4]

The comparison of the answers given at stage 1 and 2 illustrates the progress instrumental morality represents within the preconventional level. At the second stage friends are recognized as co–instrumentalists in the great game of the survival of the fittest. School-age children, we see, make better capitalists than good little socialists. The seedbed for socialist indoctrination is adolescence.

---

[4]    R. L. Selman, *The Growth of Interpersonal Understanding* (New York: Academic Press, 1980).

Since we equivocate when we talk of indoctrination, this is a good time to remember that the stages depict qualitative not quantitative change. Moral development, according to the constructivist tradition, is not the result of learning new things. It makes sense to think that gaining new knowledge or being affected by cultural influences contributes to human development. But a new stage, even in the "soft" understanding of stages, indicates a reconstruction of an old structure in a qualitatively different mode of expression. Development is not, essentially, a matter of amassing new facts or new moral opinions. It is a sequence of new ways of dealing with both. In a certain sense, each stage is a new piece of software, a new computer program that makes it possible to treat the same basic information in a more sophisticated way.

Consequently, two children at stage 2, who have been influenced by the radically different atmosphere and moral opinions of their environments, might give opposite answers to questions about the moral obligation to help others. But their answers will be woven on the same loom. A child raised in a generous family where mutual help is emphasized will think: "I should be willing to help others so that they will be willing to help me." Another child raised in a selfish family will say: "Others only think of themselves so I have to look out for me." The solutions are contradictory, but each of them depends on the same kind of reasoning to analyse the facts of moral experience.

## Moral Progress or Decline?

At play age, children understood evil as something that "fell from on high" when they dared to thwart parental prohibitions. Now that they are older, they deal with the facts of their moral experience quite differently. "Good" is the pleasant and beneficial consequence of their own cleverness. "Evil" comes from their lack of astuteness. Good and evil are, basically, a matter of skilfulness or lack of skill in using the tools apt to procure the "good life."

Through their industry and cleverness, school-age children manage to escape the fatalism of the moral vision of preschool children. They know by experience that even the big and powerful do not always carry the day. Granted, they always have the last word in the preconventional world of children. However, before they utter it, clever young negotiators find a way to manoeuvre to their advantage. They will approach both their father and mother and bargain to get the best deal possible by playing off the liberal concessions of one against the other. In other situations they will prepare an alibi or buy off a witness in advance. If caught red-handed, they will plead extenuating circumstances or suggest a compomise. When found guilty, they will negotiate a more benign sentence by skilfully weighing which consequences have the least disastrous effects on their comfort.

Adults with great moral integrity might conclude that the imperial mores of older children represent the quintessence of the moral duplicity and decline that Emmanual Kant called radical evil.[5] There is, obviously, the possibility that the moral instrumentalism of stage 2 will degenerate into freely chosen attitudes and ways of behaving. Since a morally clear–sighted and responsible supporting culture is conscious of this danger, it insistently signals to the chil-

---

5    O. Reboul, *Kant et le problème du mal* (Montréal: Les Presses de l'Université de Montréal, 1971), pp. 79–119.

dren as they move into the pre–adolescent phase that members of the family circle are not happy with the instrumental
role the children assign them. Those who are close to them
challenge the validity of the attitude that pays attention to
nothing but their own self–interest in the process of making
decisions. They demand that the children manifest a higher
degree of mutuality in their interpersonal relations. They
make them realize they are waiting for them to be worthy
of their confidence. They encourage the development of a
close friendship with a buddy because this is the privileged
means for passing on to the next stage. Unless we adopt a
rigid structuralist position and pay no attention to the facts
of life in the family and at school, we cannot deny the influences these cultural messages have on development.

In itself, however, the morality of stage 2 is not a morality in decline. Those who interpret it negatively confuse
the structure of the instrumental experience of moral existence with specific moral content. Anyone who knowingly
and consciously cheats another for reasons of self–interest
chooses a content that he or she knows to be immoral. Depending on the case, the content can be labelled inauthen-
ticity or insincerity, a falsehood or a lie, calumny or
spiteful innuendo. The structural egocentricity of the imperial stage is something quite different. Piaget says that this
egocentricity is a kind of systematic and unconscious perspective illusion.[6] We are dealing with a narcissism

---

[6]    J. Piaget, *Le langage et la pensée de l'enfant* (Neuchâtel:
Delachaux et Niestlé, 1923), p. 68. The chapter from which this quote is
taken has not been translated in: *The Language and Thought of the Child*
(New York: Meridian Books, 1955).

without Narcissus. Although children act in their own interests, they have no ulterior motives in doing so.

Structural instrumentalism represents, moreover, a developmental advance for young, school–age moralists. To appreciate it we have to bracket the unpleasant social consequences, that is, the treatment of others as means to an end. As we mentioned above, it is this undesirable by-product of instrumentalism that prompts family members to demand a higher degree of mutuality from the pre–adolescent. If, on the contrary, we pay attention to the quality of the relationship of the subject to the moral object, we see that, from this point of view, instrumentalism indicates a significant qualitative leap.

Older children, in fact, begin to emerge from their purely objectivist, external and materialist vision of good and evil. They no longer conceive of evil as something that grabs them or as a trap into which they fall. They now take part in the elaboration of the moral object. Good and evil are the fruits of their competence and incompetence. Not only do they participate in shaping the moral object, but they devote themselves to doing it through certain kinds of interactions with others. They are never the only ones involved when they do right or wrong. Despite all that is said, especially in regard to sexual experience, there is no "solitary sin" beyond the impulsive stage. The instrumental experience of morality already contains the first, imperfect beginnings of the interpersonal reality of every moral act. Imperial subjects shape right and wrong by their skill or lack of skill in dealing with others.

In milieux which have mastered the art of moral education, people will not be too quick to react to the instru-

mental manoeuvres of the young. They will give them time
to differentiate clearly their role as subjects, even if this
means that children often think of themselves before thinking of others. They will recognize a sense of self–sufficien-
cy and competence in the young and cultivate these
qualities. In the mid–eighties, Canadian television showed
a series of vignettes prepared by the Mormons. A young
child comes into the house with a big smile on his or her
face and proudly announces to the unseen parent that he or
she has been successful in some task, school test or sports
challenge. The viewers then hear the kill–joy voice of the
parent, not approving, thanking or praising, but flatly recalling how much remains to be done, or lamenting the fact
that the child only took second place. These vignettes very
cleverly made the adult population aware of its primary educational responsibility to confirm and celebrate the competence of older children.

To put the finishing touches on our own vignette about
the imperial stage, we should remember that the moral subject functioned at the preconventional level. Despite the
unquestionable progress represented by stage 2, this moral
structure must still be labelled anomie (without laws). We
may object that the family imposes rules in stage 1 and that
the family, school and the peer group do so in stage 2. Don't
these rules function as the law for them? Yes, they do. In
the child's moral existence, however, the rules do not have
the status of conventions or laws. They do not function as
commonly accepted rational norms of how one should behave for the sake of the common good. On the one hand,
children do not perceive that the rules have a sound basis.
What they know are the immediate consequences. On the
other hand, they do not think of the rules as established "for

the sake of the common good." The idea of the good of a community of persons sharing a history is not yet part of their mental and affective universe. The rules only function as limitations to their individual pleasure and freedom of action. The construction of the concept of a community is something yet to be achieved.

## From Hedonism to Utilitarianism

Eric Volant quotes a text of Herbert Spencer, a utilitarian ethicist of the second half of the nineteenth century, which illustrates the close links between the hedonist and utilitarian ethical models.[7] Spencer maintains that all ethical theories concur in qualifying behaviour that brings beneficial results as good, and behaviour that has harmful consequences as bad. According to Spencer the criterion of moral judgment should be the happiness or unhappiness produced by each individual's conduct. Drunkenness, he says, would not be bad were it not for the deplorable consequences it has for the individual and his family. Theft would not be criminal if "it gave as much pleasure to the one who loses as to the one who steals."

Just as the instrumentalism of the imperial stage represents an improvement over the heteronomy of the impulsive stage in terms of the preconventional level, so utilitarianism represents an advance beyond hedonism in terms of an individualistic conception of ethics. Like hedonism, utilitarianism thinks of ethics as the art of attaining individual satisfaction. In the hedonistic model, the end envisaged by the moral project is understood in terms of the

---

[7]　E. Volant, *Des morales: Crises et impératifs* (Montréal and Paris: Éditions Paulines et Médiaspaul, 1985), pp. 92–93.

experience of pleasure. Discernment is focussed, therefore, directly on pleasure, pain and their hierarchization.

These same preoccupations appear in the western utilitarian ethics produced in England in the eighteenth and nineteenth centuries. Even if the honour of having invented the term "utilitarianism," and having systematized utilitarian doctrine belongs to John Stuart Mill (1806–1873), the paternity of the utilitarian model can be traced back to Jeremy Bentham (1749–1832). Bentham is rightly famous for his "arithmetic of pleasures," a calculated technique for the pursuit of "authentic pleasure." Unlike Epicurus, Bentham sees no qualitative distinction between one pleasure and another. He bases his calculation on a set of six variables.[8] Moral agents are able to make a correct choice from among possible courses of action by adding and comparing the different quantities of pleasure: duration, intensity, certitude, proximity, fruitfulness and purity. From this point of view, the Benthamian art of balancing the pleasure budget does not even have the quality of Epicurus' system. Mill is more refined than Bentham on this point. His qualitative analyses of pleasure return to those of Greek philosophy.[9] Bentham's insistence on a mathematical exactitude, however, tells us more about utilitarianism's advance beyond hedonism.

---

[8]  J. Bentham, *Deontology* (Oxford: Clarendon Press, 1984), particularly pp. 130–153.

[9]  J. S. Mill, "Utilitarianism," in J. M. Robson (ed.), *Essays on Ethics, Religion and Society* (Toronto: University of Toronto Press, 1969), pp. 209–226.

Epicureanism concentrates on the pleasures *experienced*. It puts the emphasis on the quality of satisfaction that each action procures. Utilitarianism thinks in terms of the pleasures *won* by its own effort. Like children entranced by their new-found ability to produce effects, utilitarians take more interest in the calculation of the doer than pleasure in the finished product. *Homo ludens* has yielded his place to *homo faber*. For the first, good or evil is gauged by the measure of pleasure or pain experienced. For the second, the measure is how efficiently the action produces joy. The focus is on what procures happiness, on what comes before its consequence. We are dealing with an ethics where the means have priority over the end.

Bentham confines his calculation of the utility of acts to the individual concerned. Mill replaces this egotistical utilitarianism with a universal utilitarianism. Without surrendering a concern for the individual, he adds an interest in a plurality of persons. He adds a seventh variable to his arithmetic for the maximization of happiness: the number of persons who experience the pleasure. We should not deceive ourselves about this extension to the interests of the largest possible number of individuals. When Mill thinks of the "greatest amount of happiness altogether," he is not designating a value that transcends each of the individuals concerned. Public interest to utilitarians is no more than the sum of private interests or the coincidence of individual interests. The difference is quantitative: the same pleasure enjoyed by many individuals instead of only by one.

In the twentieth century, the utilitarian school has widened its notion still further. They call the orthodox "act utilitarians." They ask: "What effect will this act I do in this situation have on the general balance of good and evil?"

Some of today's utilitarians claim to follow a "rule utilitarianism." They ask a different question: "What effect would this action have on the balance of good and evil if performed by everyone, everywhere?"[10] In this interpretation the question begins to take on the shape of Kant's categorical imperative: "Act only according to that maxim by which you can at the same time will that it should become a universal law." Do these latest formulations mean that we are witnessing a transition from a pragmatic consequentialism to an idealist deontology?

François Grégoire puts a group of moral systems that he labels "scientific" in the same classification as Epicureanism and utilitarianism.[11] This twinning of classical doctrines based on a philosophical conception of nature and contemporary doctrines dependent on a scientific discipline is instructive. It brings out another way in which the contemporary utilitarian model duplicates the moral experience of a stage 2 subject.

Whether we are dealing with an ethics based on psychophysiological views (Freud) or an ethics based on sociological analysis (Durkheim), they both have the same aim: to decode the laws of physical nature. When science gets that far, human beings will have acquired a method to calculate the optimum return. They will be able to foresee what each action yields, and have a foolproof technique for happiness. Science will replace ethics which is only a provisional regime of uncertainty. This is the adult version of

---

[10]  See W. K. Frankena, *Ethics* (Englewood Cliffs: Prentice–Hall, 1973), pp. 35–43.

[11]  F. Grégoire, *Les grandes doctrines morales* (Paris: Presses Universitaires de France, 1967), pp. 74–90.

the attitude of pre–adolescents who think that, once every-thing that can be classified has been classified, they can rule over the demystified empires they have conquered with the know–how of a computer.

## The Merits of Moral Pragmatism

Minimizing the contribution utilitarianism makes to ethics is a costly error that opens the way to idealist moral systems that are unable to engender results that are well adjusted to the real needs of the persons we are. Utilitarian-ism counts on an unalterable human exigency: in playing our role as concrete operator we cause effects that affect us, first of all. However an ethical system conceives, discerns and carries out the good, it will be inadequate unless it takes into account the consequences of the acts of the indi-viduals concerned, and the effect on themselves first of all. People who are motivated by an ideal such as human soli-darity to help someone else, without paying any attention to the negative effects their generosity might have on their commitments, health and family life, delude themselves about the morality of their decision. It is better, as popular wisdom warns, "to let well enough alone." Moral discern-ment cannot be reduced to the calculation of effects but, if you ignore them, you place the validity of your decision in doubt. Only the foolish do not take time to consider the consequences of their decisions.

The scientific aspect of calculating the effects is anoth-er contribution to moral reflection. Many moralists under-rate it. Some think that the science of primary causes does away with the science of secondary causes. Others, more prosaically, ignore both the method and the facts. In both cases they try to discern good and evil by imagining the human reality affected by action rather than by knowing it. A moral evaluation of "just price" that is based on profit, and disregards the costs of investment, research and marketing has no chance of being right because it pays no attention to the economic laws that constitute current commercial practice.

Moral discernment is a human task. As such, it presupposes the two primary operations of the mind: an accurate apprehension of what is, and the comprehension of what is apprehended. Scientific investigation makes a contribution to these two initial moves of the moral subject. On their precision depends the correctness of the two following operations: the moral judgment and the moral decision to act. Whether they are professional moralists or not, people who knowingly refuse to acquire adequate cognitive competence (proportionate to their capacity, the seriousness of what is involved, the urgency of the decision, etc.) before making a moral judgment are guilty of negligence and, therefore, responsible for the harm that results.

## Insignificance of the Utilitarian Order

As Hannah Arendt emphasizes, the fundamental problem of utilitarianism is that there is nothing to justify the utilitarian order itself.[12] The business of being human is reduced to the category of the useful. Doesn't usefulness, taken as the meaning of life, breed a sense of absurdity? What meaning can an existence dedicated to producing useful things have? Does the value of human beings depend entirely on the calculation of what they produce? Is there

---

[12]  H. Arendt, *The Human Condition* (Chicago: University of Chicago Press, 1965), pp. 153–159.

nothing in them worth being recognized and loved except what makes them useful? Even if they wear themselves out, body and soul, living according to utilitarian morality, those who are bright and courageous enough to ask about the content of their meaning–making cannot help but feel "the unbearable lightness of being" described by the Czech novelist, Milan Kundera.[13] Since they have been true to their vision they cannot be charged with being bad human beings. But there is so much more waiting to be born than what they have engendered!

The insignificance of the utilitarian order becomes, perhaps, even more obvious in its scientific version. Here its deterministic and mechanistic understanding of human nature is clearly exposed. Far from being an autocreative power, human liberty is the by–product of our present ignorance. If the day ever comes when we have an exhaustive knowledge of our acts, the word "choose" will be dropped from our vocabulary. "The best of all possible worlds" described by Aldous Huxley will replace the uncertain world of freedom in which we are presently condemned to live.

### Religious Mercantilism and the Merchant God

Walter Vogels has clearly shown that what is at stake in the Book of Job is the issue of "how to speak correctly about God."[14] In the epilogue Yahweh addresses one of Job's friends: "I burn with anger against you and your two friends for not speaking truthfully about me as my servant

---

[13]   M. Kundera, *The Unbearable Lightness of Being* (New York: Harper & Row, 1984).

[14]   W. Vogels, *Reading and Preaching the Bible: A New Semiotic Approach* (Wilmington: M. Glazier, 1986), pp. 80–106.

Job has done" (42:7). These three men, however, spoke about God in the traditional language of retribution. Where they went wrong was in conceiving all relations with God on this model: if Job is having trouble, he must have sinned. They have a banker's view of religion and ethics.[15] Samuel Terrien writes that "religion is a business transaction for them, humility an insurance policy, and morality a coin that buys peace of mind and prosperity. . . . They are not defending God but their need for security."[16] God and his creature are partners in a business deal.

This religious anthropocentrism, which is so typical of stage 2,[17] is a close relative of the pietist outlook. It adds the element of haggling with God. When the faithful try to manipulate the divinity, utilitarian relationships are transposed to the religious domain. The use of scapulars and the wearing of medals for unfailing protection, the nine first Fridays that guarantee reconciliation at the hour of death, prayers that work by virtue of their words alone, promises made to God in exchange for favours, merits that God is obliged to honour *de condigno* — all this trading that scandalized Luther is congenital to utilitarian meaning–making.

Like the ethics that called it forth, this sacred mercantilism can be tempered by other factors that keep it from degenerating into religious Machiavellianism. Who hasn't felt traces of certain venal attitudes towards God in times of pressing need? When these feelings characterize the attitude taken towards religion or the Christian faith, they

---

[15]  J. Steinman, *Le livre de Job* (Paris: Cerf, 1955), p. 307.

[16]  S. Terrien, *Job* (Neuchâtel: Delachaux et Niestlé), 1963), p. 41.

[17]  J. Fowler, "Life/Faith Patterns," in J. Berryman (ed.), *Life Maps* (Waco: Winston Press, 1978), p. 51.

corrupt religion by turning it into superstition. This apes religion and faith by establishing a link with a suprahuman world. Unlike religion and faith, however, superstition tries to snatch their secrets away from the mysterious forces through divination, and uses magic to constrain them unfailingly to produce extraordinary effects for their benefit. This utilitarian superstition, which eats and gnaws away at the religious attitude from within, is the most serious deformation of religious mercantilism. The superstitious, not content to reduce God to a supplier, turn to the practices of witchcraft in order to subjugate God to their desires. The popularity astrology, necromancy, tarot card reading and the occult in all its forms enjoy in our consumer society says much about the utilitarian ethics they represent.

Chapter Three

# Fusional Stage
# and Loyalty Ethics

## Adolescent Moratorium

Most specialists in human development accept Erikson's definition of adolescence as a psychosocial moratorium granted the young to enable them to become adults. They agree that puberty signals its beginning. But harmony among the experts ends there.

People have always known that life is made up of cycles, and that puberty marks the beginning of one of them. In societies less complex than our own, the limits within which adolescence is lived are usually tightly and clearly defined.[1] In post–industrial countries, however, these limits are much less precise. On the one hand, the changes of puberty, caused by the enormous increase of sexual hormones, start earlier in most of our children than they did in

---

[1]    B. B. Whiting and J. W. M. Whiting, *Children of Six Cultures* (Cambridge: Harvard University Press, 1975).

the past. It has been calculated, for example, that the age of puberty for girls has dropped four months in every ten years during the last century. This adds up to three years and four months between 1880 and 1980.[2] On the other hand, this statistical decrease allows for considerable variations from one child to another. It is normally accepted that pubescent changes begin in girls between the ages of eight and 13, and in boys between the ages of 10 and 15. There are many exceptions to this scale. One boy in a thousand begins his pubescent period at the age of eight for example, while the same proportion of boys do not enter puberty until they are 24 years old. Similarly, the psychological changes of puberty are completed in one year for some while they take five and a half years for others.[3] As if these variations were not upsetting enough, the social referents of adolescence differ according to cultures, social classes and historical periods.

It comes as no surprise, therefore, that researchers in development are very imprecise about when the third stage, that begins around the time of adolescence, actually starts. Most authors think of a period extending from 12 or 13 to 18 or 19, when adolescents are "teenagers."

## Hypothetico-deductive Aptitude

The concrete, reversible operations have usually been mastered during pre-adolescence. Logical thought can now enter its final stage involving the formal operations. Jean

---

[2] A. C. Peterson, "Can Puberty Come Any Earlier?" in *Psychology Today,* Vol. 12, No. 9, 1980, p. 45.

[3] A. C. Peterson, "Those Gangly Years," in *Psychology Today,* Vol. 21, No. 9, 1987, pp. 28–34.

Piaget and Barbel Inhelder insist that the principal characteristic of formal operational thought is its application to the "possible" rather than the "actual." [4] The formal operators are no longer satisfied with organizing concrete data by classification. They proceed from these classifications to formulate hypotheses that go far beyond factual observations. They then deduce conclusions that have a value irrespective of their actual, concrete truth. The actual takes second place to the possible. The actual is only an example of what might be, or a subset of a larger whole. Scientific thinking comes to birth.

The acquisition of the hypothetico–deductive aptitude opens up a new horizon of comprehension. Now subjects can construct the world propositionally, hypothetically, inferentially and abstractly. They possess a research tool which enables them to go beyond the exercises in classification that held their attention in the previous period. Now they can take up the problem where they left it and, on the basis of the facts, erect the series of relationships they suggest. Then they can use either logic or experimentation to figure out which series of relationships are verifiable and which are not. Adolescents who have reached the level of formal operations are builders of potential worlds and systems. They know how to sketch out an overall plan. They think about thinking. They even construct a new epistemology in which what is outside them is not necessarily real,

---

[4]     See D. G. Boyle, *A Students' Guide to Piaget* (Oxford: Pergamon, 1969), p. 92; H. Ginsburg and S. Opper, *Piaget's Theory of Intellectual Development: An Introduction* (Englewood Cliffs: Prentice–Hall, 1969), pp. 202–203.

and what is inside them is not necessarily unreal. Reality is sometimes more internal than external.

Since this cognitive revolution applies not only to things but to the realities of human life, it helps to change the way adolescents view society. Psychology often neglects this cognitive factor, even though it is really more decisive than the physiological and cultural referents of puberty. Certainly the sensual empowerment and the genitalization of sexuality create attractions that draw the young out of their preconventional loneliness. However, without cognitive distancing from the concreteness of the facts, adolescents would be unable to move away from a structurally egotistical perspective.

Once the self has taken some distance from itself, it no longer has the solidity of a concrete and implacable given. The concreteness in which the subjects have been submerged up to now is objectified (from *objicere:* literally, "throw in front," "set against," as in the German word *Gegenstand*). The subjects are no longer their needs. They have needs. Recognized as objects, these become material for their attention and consideration. The new subjects have the leisure to co-ordinate their own needs with the needs of other subjects–who–are–distinct–from–their–needs. Their differentiation from the world of needs is such that the new integration takes the form of a "relationship to." Their formal operation of thinking gives them the ability to undertake the formation of interpersonal relationships — a human reality that they have not understood until now.

The hypotheses that they spontaneously elaborate about the self–in–relation open adolescents to the possibilities of autotransformation. They take a deeper look at the

other than in the good old imperial times of "I see you —
you see me" simple reciprocity. Adolescents adopt what
constructivists call "third–person perspectives." The distance they take in relation to their self–in–relation allows
each of them to say, "I see you seeing me"; "I see me as you
see me"; "I see you seeing me seeing you." This ability to
"see themselves looking," to stand back from what they and
others are doing and look at themselves as third parties is
the basis of the self–in–relation. It leads to the construction
of a diversified network of interpersonal relationships.

Freed from their enslaving concreteness, subjects operating at the formal level add a historical perspective to
their self–understanding that was lacking earlier. They are
able to reconstruct the expansion of time before the present
period. They can anticipate a personal and interpersonal future based on the projected transformations of the self–in–
relation.

## Self–in–Conversation

The new situation of the adolescent self disturbs the
unilateral perception of the self young people had acquired.
If identity is essentially the expression of the constitutive
self–understanding that subjects have of themselves, this is
obviously put in question by the adolescent perspective. A
new, refreshing question comes to the fore: "Who am I in
the sight of others?" This is why Erikson thinks that the
psychosocial task of adolescents is the acquisition of a
sense of their own identity that can withstand the confusion
of roles.

Individuals succeed in this important task to the degree
that they gain confidence that their sense of self, of "same-

ness," is recognized and appreciated by others despite all the changes that it undergoes. This is fundamentally what the quest for the Holy Grail becomes for adolescents: the community's confirmation of their historical identity. To the degree that the culture in which adolescents are embedded does not reward this enterprise, adolescents do not really possess this identity. As Kegan points out, the self resides somewhere between the individual and the other. Young adolescents, torn between the two, successively fluctuate between alienation and autonomy.

In their quest for self–recognition adolescents turn into "talkers." Conversation becomes their preferred occupation because they are trying to define themselves in the plurality of familiar voices. The old saying, "much talk, little action," applies to adolescents. They are looking for their own coherence in what others say about them. Even their "falling in love" in an effort to satisfy their desires is partly a quest for self–definition. By projecting their own diffused self–image on others, who are idealized and romanticized, adolescents hope to clarify their own identity. That is why, Erikson remarks, "so much of young love is conversation."[5]

Strictly speaking, adolescents do not have interpersonal relationships. They are relationships to others. The self has become a shared reality. To call this new equilibrium of stage 3 "interpersonal," as Kegan does, causes confusion, especially for people who have been influenced by personalist philosophy where "interpersonal" carries rich connotations of intimacy and sharing between autonomous

---

[5]　E. H. Erikson, *Identity: Youth and Crisis* (New York: W. W. Norton, 1968), p. 132.

individuals and presupposes that the relations to others have been "object–ified." At the third stage, however, the equilibrium of the self is not interpersonal but, as Kegan admits, fusional. I have, therefore, used this adjective to identify stage 3.

In their effort to make sense of themselves relationally adolescents clan together. They are looking for exclusive groups where they can find ideas and people they can trust and to whom they can give their allegiance. Adolescents are defined only by *insiders*, by those who know and appreciate them. *Outsiders*, for all practical purposes, do not exist. They play no part in the process of "meaning–making." In the eyes of adolescents they literally are insignificant. Hence Erikson suggests that loyalty is the characteristic virtue of this age group. Despite the inevitable contradictions between the value systems and ideologies of the various communities to which they belong, adolescents need to establish and maintain some freely undertaken loyalties. Adolescents often cultivate a sharp sense of duty, truth, sincerity, authenticity and dedication in the select circles of the family, school, peer group, sports team or church that define them. These are certainly integrative virtues, but practising them and maintaining the "happy medium" is a delicate matter!

The supporting culture should recognize and nurture the adolescent need to share subjective experience. Adolescents become dysfunctional in an environment which lacks the attitudes their meaning–making needs. The extensive literature on juvenile delinquency is a sad commentary on the megastructures of institutions whose gigantic anonymity cannot incite adolescent allegiance.

While those close to adolescents should meet their need for fusion, they should also cautiously invite them to take their distance from the group and assert themselves. Political parties or religious sects which take advantage of the insecurity of this period to recruit followers are likely to foster an intolerant, puritanical fanaticism in them. They are guilty towards these adolescent individuals of *lèse-identité*. They deprive society of free citizens who are capable of establishing a social contract and living up to it.

## Morality of Interpersonal Expectations

One of Kohlberg's subjects, a 10-year-old boy who was given the code name "Joe," was asked, "Why shouldn't we steal from a store?" He answered, "It isn't good to steal from a store. It's against the law. Someone might see you and call the police." When Joe was asked the same question when he was 17, he answered, "It's a question of law. One of our rules is that we try to protect people and their property. . . . It's something we need in our society. If we didn't have these laws, people would steal. They wouldn't have to work for a living and our society would lose its balance."

This response of the adolescent Joe is peppered with possessive pronouns. Joe manifestly identifies with his group. The group's needs, rules and well-being are his own. Without his community, everything, including his identity, would tumble into chaos. That is why he endorses the viewpoint of his community. The rules and expectations of the group are internalized. They become his, not through psychic reconstruction as in the case of the impulsive subject, but through social identification. Since the fusional subject is defined by his group, its conventions are his. This is the backdrop of the conventional level of moral development.

It should be noted that passage to this level is made possible by the subject's cognitive aptitude to construct abstract systems, in this case, a community system. Without this logical prerequisite, they would not be able to conceive of others and themselves as "parts of a whole." Adolescents who have access to formal operations are able to think of social functions as abstract entities separate from the specific persons who carry them out. They also realize that members of the community enjoy certain privileges that go beyond the actual exercise of this or that privilege (for example, assurance that they will be protected by their group and its representatives, in case of need). Without these hypothetical–deductive aptitudes an individual, whether adolescent or adult, would be unable to move beyond the preconventional level.

Psychoanalytical tradition adds fuel to Kohlberg's fire. In his first theory about the psychic system, Freud emphasized the authority of the superego *(Uber–Ich):* the internal reconstruction of parental prohibitions during the resolution of the Oedipus complex. In his second theory, another relatively independent intrapsychic formation appears: the ego ideal *(Ichideal).*[6] Even though psychoanalysts do not agree on how the ego ideal should be interpreted, many see it as an adolescent construction. They define this authority as the interior image that individuals have of themselves when they are trying to be and to act in accord with the expectations of those they love. The ego ideal, therefore, designates a differentiation of the psychic system. It helps

---

[6]  L. E. Hinsie and R. J. Campbell, *Psychiatric Dictionary* (New York: Oxford University Press, 1976), p. 252.

in the elaboration of the moral judgments we encounter in the protocols of stage 3 subjects.

Sometimes Kohlberg defines this stage of moral development as interpersonal conformity and sometimes as interpersonal expectation. The first term applies to activity, the second to the attitude from which it proceeds. The fusional self thinks of right and wrong in terms of what those who are near and dear expect of him or her. To respond positively to their expectations is good, to respond negatively, or not at all, is bad. This is what Kohlberg calls a "nice girl, nice boy" morality. The reinterpretation of the sequence of development in 1973 makes these qualifications seem less appropriate since it is hard to believe that adolescents think of conformity to the expectations of the tribe as a matter of nice manners. The idea, nonetheless, is accurate. The applause of the gallery does, indeed, define adolescent "good deeds."

At this moral stage individuals do not see others for themselves. They look at them to see if they are looking their way with praise in their eyes. Sam Keen writes that adolescents are "always looking into the mirror of another's eyes, searching for a sign of approval."[7] He adds that the inner eyes of fusional individuals are turned towards the tribunal of conscience, where they try to present their case in the best possible light in order to win a "not guilty" verdict. The loss of their reputation, that is, the favourable opinion others have of them, means the loss of their personal identity. The self–love of these individuals is nurtured only by the approbation of the group that defines them.

----

[7]     S. Keen, *The Passionate Life: Stages of Loving* (San Francisco: Harper and Row, 1983), p. 60.

Kohlberg draws out of these moral protocols a form of moral judgment that corresponds quite well to the fidelity which Erikson describes as the characteristic virtue of adolescence. Stage 3 moral judgments are judgments of attachment and loyalty to their comrades and the cause they hold in common. Justice is seen as the ability to adopt this third party perspective which is the ego ideal, the self–representation of subjects trying to live up to the expectations of those who are important to them. This reciprocity of the utopian third person no longer has the individualistic and concrete character of the elementary reciprocity of the imperial stage. Reciprocity idealized by familiar voices structures the subject's identity. We could call it *esprit de corps*.

Since most adolescents establish reciprocal links with more than one defining group, this moral position can be uncomfortable at times. Inevitably the various groups to which youths belong express different and even contradictory expectations. An adolescent girl might think to herself, "If I resist my boyfriend's sexual advances, my family and my church group will applaud but the kids at school and my friends will think I'm stupid." Once again, the choice she makes has nothing to do with her moral stage. The form of judgment put forward and the action that follows from it is the same in both cases. Right and wrong will be the consequence of her conformity to the dominant defining group.

At this stage, the best our adolescents can do is to synthesize the information and conventions transmitted by the groups monopolizing their affection. That is why James Fowler calls this the "synthetic–conventional" stage. This synthesizing is a difficult task because adolescents have not yet objectified the underlying ideology of each group for the purpose of analysis. Because the fusional self is unable to examine critically the values involved, the self must be satisfied with meeting the expectations of this group and that as best he or she can. Fowler observes that two strategies are used to achieve this. Adolescents either compartmentalize by changing their behaviour code as they pass from one group to the next or they create a hierarchy of moral authorities.

## Weakness and Strength of Conventional Bonds

Adolescents judge right and wrong by a system of directive ideas that are held together by the all–embracing logic and utopian conviction of conventional attachment and not, as at the preconventional level, by practical experience nor, as at the postconventional level, by an internal coherence.[8] Though it may look very reassuring to the fusional self, this characteristic moral perspective of the adolescent truce can leave adolescents with serious bruises, as we mentioned earlier.

The moral dignity of stage 3 individuals is located, as far as they are concerned, in the favourable opinion of others. They consider themselves as good as the reputation they have among their peers, especially among those they hold in high regard. We know how easily defamation, whether true or false, can damage their right to a good name. We also know how a malicious rumour can sow discord among close friends.[9] Adolescents whose identity depends on the unconditional support of the culture in which they are embedded can suffer enormously from this. These

---

[8]    E. H. Erikson, *The Challenge of Youth* (Garden City: Doubleday, 1965), pp. 1–28.

obnoxious linguistic practices can destroy the moral fibre of the self–in–conversation whose certitudes are limited to what the voices of the approving group around him or her have to say. We would be shocked to learn how many adolescent suicides originate in words that are, quite literally, dipped in poison.

Even if fusional subjects no longer think of leadership as an authoritarian function (stage 1) or the mediator of reciprocal interests (stage 2), they still see it as something needed in the homogeneous communities to which they belong. The function of the leader, Robert Selman explains, is to marshal the group's solidarity, to help it structure itself into a whole, and to promote a sense of community among its members.[10] Fusional subjects are still very dependent on their leaders. Consequently, they are badly shaken in their moral convictions when one leader or other abandons or betrays the cause.

Lastly, we should note the imminent danger of illuminism and religious and political fanaticism that threatens individuals whose moral vision is so radically anchored in the affective and psychodynamic needs of the self. In a time of rapid social change like ours, we are witnessing the spontaneous generation of small sects whose members receive the charism of "tongues of fire" that changes them from one day to the next into apocalyptic preachers. This phenomenon is typical of the moral and religious distress of stage 3.

---

[9]    See R. L. Rosnow and G. A. Fine, *Rumors and Gossip: The Social Psychology of Hearsay* (New York: Elsevier, 1976); P. A. M. Spacks, *Gossip* (New York: A. A. Knopf, 1985).

[10]    R. L. Selman, *The Growth of Interpersonal Understanding* (New York: Academic Press, 1980), p. 118.

However fragile the evolutionary truce of the adolescent passage, its morality of solidarity does, nonetheless, represent a step forward. In fact it is a giant step, because it is a transition not only from one stage to another, but from one level to the next. For the first time these individuals recognize an order of normative values that goes beyond the pleasurable *(bonum concupiscibile)* and the useful *(bonum utile)*. Obviously, personal pleasures and interests are not excluded since the fusional self shares in the good that the group holds in common. However, this "common good" is no longer thought of as a simple accumulation of particular goods. It has acquired a transcendent quality that represents a considerable advance in the process of decentralizing the individual. At stage 3, individual satisfactions, however they are conceived, do not constitute the moral norm. Moral existence is lived under the sign of interpersonal expectations. Moral judgment and commitment ultimately flow from them.

Individuals can now take significant distance from their persona to adopt a third person point of view in evaluating their needs in relation to the demands of the group. They can simultaneously see themselves functioning in the group as observer and as observed. The basis of their personal dignity is thus enlarged. The dignity of "subject–in–relation" is added to the dignity of "subject" acquired in the previous stage. The individual is no longer wedged between a series of dyadic relations that are independent from one another and that always involve particular interests. The self is effectively in communion with a larger network of people. Their sharing together establishes an existential matrix in which the meaning–making of life is elaborated.

## Loyalty Model

If you check the table of contents of a *History of Moral Doctrines,* it is unlikely that you will find a chapter on the ethical model corresponding to the moral stage of conformity to interpersonal expectations. French personalism, which was as much an opposition to fascism as it was to communism, is something quite different. The philosophical systems which would seem to correspond most closely to Kohlberg's second level of moral development are generally thematizations of the fourth stage. There is nothing surprising in this for, as we shall see, the independent truce at the second level corresponds more closely to the realism of adult experience than the typically fusional truce of adolescence. On the other hand, the utopian character of the stage 3 vision is probably more appealing than the institutional accommodation of the following stage. Whatever the comparative appeal of these two conventional stages, what reader has not recognized the characteristics of well-known moral discourses in the preceding descriptions?

This form of morality has found at least one contemporary theoretician in the American philosopher, Josiah Royce. In 1908 Royce published *The Philosophy of Loyalty,*[11] based on a course in ethics he gave at Harvard in 1906. This book has been the object of renewed interest recently. It is noteworthy that this book is presented as a criticism of the individualistic and utilitarian pragmatism that William James, Royce's faithful friend and colleague, defended.[12]

---

[11]   J. Royce, *The Philosophy of Loyalty* (New York: Hafner, 1971).
[12]   *Ibid.,* pp. 51–98 and 301–348.

There is no doubt that Royce's concept of loyalty represents an ethical model. Loyalty, says Royce, is a "way of viewing the moral world"; "the first ethical principle or the moral law itself"; "the heart of all the virtues, the central duty amongst all duties"; "the chief amongst all the moral goods of . . . life"; "the fulfilment of the whole moral law."[13] In what does it consist? The basic, most decisive and enlightening definition is given right at the beginning: "the willing and practical and thoroughgoing devotion of a person to a cause."[14] Royce himself noted that this definition contains the three characteristics of loyalty.[15] We shall examine each of these three elements structuring the model, one after the other. Royce returned to these and deepened them in each of the "lectures" that make up his work.

In the beginning of every moral process stands the Cause, not Pleasure or Utility. This is the first value. It is larger than our private self; it stands on its own; and our private interests are subordinated to it.[16] Until we discover a cause to which to give ourselves, we are in a conflictual situation: inside we find the contradictory desires of our will and, on the outside, a social plan that demands our submission. The identification and choice of a cause resolves this "paradox of ordinary existence" by unifying our motives, our particular ideas and plans, by harmonizing the internal and the external.[17] The sovereign good that the moral law of loyalty promotes is, then, the cause, "the

---

13  *Ibid.*, pp.16, 13 and 306, vii, 57, 15.
14  *Ibid.*, pp. 16–17. See the more refined definitions on p. 357.
15  *Ibid.*, p. 17.
16  *Ibid.*, pp. 18–20.
17  *Ibid.*, pp. 26–48.

rational unity of many minds and wills."[18] By uniting the individual to others by some sort of social bond, the cause answers the fundamental ethical question: "For what do I live?"[19] Individuals respond to the cause's call by a complete, voluntary gift of self. "Loyalty means giving the Self to the Cause," "the willing and complete identification of ... self with ... cause."[20] The cause, therefore, becomes the very conscience of individuals, that which tells them what their duty really is.[21] They become servants of the cause which unifies life by giving it a focus and a central "belief."[22]

Loyalty is complete when it engenders practical devotion to a cause, that is, an external action in favour of the cause.[23] What is the point of this action? It is intended, certainly, to establish the cause whose primary function is to unite a certain number of persons. In the more developed analysis of lectures three and four, the particular effect of loyalty is described as the growth of social confidence and loyalty towards others.[24] It is basically a matter of creating an *esprit de corps* that makes each one feel that he or she is united to the others.

### Community Solidarity

A radical need to belong to a community, to be affiliated with it, and to stand in solidarity with it runs through

---

[18] *Ibid.,* pp. 307–309. See p. 47, 52, 108, 227, 252.
[19] *Ibid.,* pp. 57 and 106–107.
[20] *Ibid.,* pp. 296–297 and 105. See p. 16–17.
[21] *Ibid.,* pp. 47 and 172–185.
[22] *Ibid.,* pp. 17, 21, 101, 252, 301–302.
[23] *Ibid.,* pp. 17–18, 21, 56.
[24] *Ibid.,* pp. 118, 138–142, 154–155.

the loyalty model from one end to the other. Royce longs for a post–individualistic situation that would favour the sharing of identities, dreams and enthusiastic commitments. Indeed, Royce's biography confirms that this interpretation is well founded.[25]

An ethics that has no place for this fundamental human aspiration would be just as doomed as one that ignores the "pleasure principle" or our responsibility for the consequences of our acts. The *animal socialis* that each of us is cannot open up or become fully itself without establishing solid community bonds with its fellow human beings. These bonds create the network of social conditions that permit groups and their individual members to reach their perfection more easily and more completely. This is the classical concept of the "common good," the sovereign good of a human community standing together in solidarity.[26] The loyalty ethic educates for the sake of the common good.

The identification of individual striving with the striving of the community of those who espouse the same cause favours the flowering of lofty moral attitudes such as hope, confidence, faith, fidelity, dedication, amiability, zeal, discipline, teachability and self–control without which the effective and lasting promotion of the common good is unthinkable. Loyalty ethics, with its virtues of community

---

25   J. Clendenning, *The Life and Thought of Josiah Royce* (Madison: University of Wisconsin Press, 1985).

26   See John XXIII, *Mater et Magistra,* 1961, No. 65; *Pacem et Terris,* 1963, No. 58; Vatican II, *Gaudium et Spes,* 1965, Nos. 26 and 74; Paul VI, *Populorum Progressio,* 1967, No. 76; John–Paul II, *Sollicitudo Rei Socialis,* 1987, No. 10.

solidarity, is popular with the "partisan heroes" of commercial and industrial organizations[27] as well as with those who give their lives for nobler causes. This was the spirituality of Thomas More whose violent death for his loyalty to the Roman cause against Henry VIII gained him the official applause (canonization) of his fellow Catholics.[28]

## Utopian Ethic

The loyalty ethical model so perfectly thematizes stage 3 morality[29] that the major problem of the fusional self, its allegiance to defining groups with contradictory ideologies, occurred quite naturally to Royce. His third lecture, which he considers of central importance, raises this major objection: since we are unable to embrace all causes, how do we reconcile the loyalty of some to this cause and of others to that cause? Let your choice of a cause be such, Royce answers, that it never contradicts the loyalty of others but serves, rather, the cause of universal loyalty. This is the famous notion of loyalty to loyalty itself.[30]

His efforts to overcome the contradictions inherent to any loyalty ethic bring out the utopian character of his model. In his plea for loyalty to loyalty Royce postulates, in effect, "a harmony of the self and the world." A loyal person need only "avoid unnecessary conflict with the

---

[27]  W. H. Whyte, *Organization Man* (New York: Simon & Schuster, 1956).

[28]  B. Byron, *Loyalty in the Spirituality of St. Thomas More* (Nieuwkoop: B. De Graaf, 1972).

[29]  Royce himself indicates that "the age for true and systematic loyalty can hardly precede adolescence." *The Philosophy of Loyalty*, p. 259.

[30]  *Ibid.*, pp. 101–146.

causes of others" in order to discover and manifest it.[31] Conflicts, which arise out of the individual's limited knowledge, are illusory, in any case.[32] Moral development consists precisely in an increased capacity to embrace more and more universal causes until the point where conflict disappears.[33]

The idea that the highest moral achievement is the disappearance of conflict is a utopian notion. Secular human experience points, rather, as we shall see, towards a sapiential art that is able to reconcile the inevitable human conflicts. Loyalty ethics has not yet, however, assimilated this experience. Under the impulse of loyalty ethics, even someone as involved in the world as Thomas More was prompted to compose *Utopia* in imitation of Plato's *The Republic*. In this Island of Nowhere, the myths of the noble savage and the classless society without private property came to birth two centuries before Jean–Jacques Rousseau and three and a half centuries before Karl Marx.[34]

In addition, Royce's speculation on "universal causes" seems to exceed his own experience. He does not, however, pay attention to what this clearly shows. Every time Royce refers to "causes" in his book they are always limited and conflictual causes such as the causes of the patriot or the soldier, the martyr, the military leader, the servant, the merchant, the samourai, the knight, of the speaker of the English parliament who sided with the members against

---

[31] *Ibid.,* pp. 123 and 133.
[32] *Ibid.,* pp. 183–185.
[33] *Ibid.,* pp. 207–209.
[34] T. More, *Utopia,* edited by E. Surtz and J. H. Hexter (New Haven: Yale University Press, 1965).

Charles I in 1642, of a member of a family, a profession, a brotherhood, a sports team, a club, a religious sect, and a political movement.[35] Is it not significant that Royce saw the vast and impersonal character of the nation as something that made it difficult to practise loyalty ethics in the United States? Individuals no longer are able to recognize their social unity in familiar forms. Does he not preach a return to a new and enlightened provincialism?[36] If the union of the States is too vast and impersonal a cause to awaken loyalty, what, then, of humanity's cause?

Some elements to resolve loyalty conflicts do emerge in Royce's thought. They foreshadow the need to go beyond the loyalty system. Loyalty's attitude towards loyalty sometimes takes the form of a defence of the veracity of one lone individual against everyone else.[37] This way of acting may serve, in Royce's perspective, to augment "social confidence." But does this rule come from the loyalty ethic? Does it not come, rather, from the self's personal integrity which, when convinced by moral evidence, is strong enough to withstand all external pressure?

## Religious Purism and "the God of Our Fathers"

In the area of religion and faith, loyalty ethics favours a purist model of the *ecclesia,* the assembly of the faithful. If there is any area where utopia is likely to become idealistic and doctrinaire, it is certainly religion. There is no danger of bumping into a flesh and bone God who will

---

[35] J. Royce, *The Philosophy of Loyalty*, pp. 17, 40, 43, 72, 102, 103–106, 183–184, 234–235, 264, 270.

[36] *Ibid.,* pp. 232–248.

[37] *Ibid.,* pp. 134–136.

hinder the Great Dream. When opposition arises, it will always be easy to write it off as the product of human weakness. As Royce expresses it, this weakness, which is an obstacle to the divinization process of humanity, only serves to reveal a Self still insufficiently dedicated to the divine cause.

The church group is thought of as a fortress that protects believers, the faithful, the pure, the pious, and the predestined against the unbelievers, the impure, the impious, and the damned. The Judeo–Christian tradition, like most religious traditions, occasionally allows this purist ecclesiology to surface. It evokes the Chosen People, the heavenly Jerusalem, the holy Body of Christ, this Church without spot or stain that has received "what God has said." Its fidelity consists in keeping this divine deposit intact. Like Royce's philosophy, this sublime vision of the Church makes it possible to use the perspective of eternity to call on the faithful to transcend themselves.[38] Its failure to pay attention to human and historical realities makes it tend, however, towards a rigid and intolerant dogmatism and, pastorally, towards a condemnation and excommunication of the world. This is the temptation of Calvinism. However, the "Lefebvre affair," and the patience Rome showed towards this "integrist" dissidence for so long, demonstrate that the purist temptation lies in wait for all the churches.[39]

The faithful, under the influence of a loyalty ethics, will spontaneously give priority to images of God that fit their vision of the world. Fowler has noted that, in stage 3

---

[38]    *Ibid.,* "Lecture VIII: Loyalty and Religion," pp. 351–398.

[39]    See *America,* Vol. 158 (1988), pp. 573–574; 602–606; Vol. 159 (1988), pp. 124–125.

protocols, "the images of God . . . are based on 'personal' qualities of the deity — for instance, God as friend, companion, 'life–line,' comforter, guide, 'mind.'"[40] These images suggest the god Joseph Moingt calls "the God of our Fathers."[41] It is the tribal God, "the God of Abraham, Isaac and Jacob." The ancient Romans spoke of the *penates,* the domestic gods who protected the city and the household. The primary function of such a divinity is to assure the permanence of the culture of embeddedness that protects our own identity. Morality and faith have a long way to travel before letting go of this god (Genesis 12:1; John 16:7). Only then will the real God emerge: "I am who I am" (Exodus 3:14).

---

[40]   J. W. Fowler, "Life/Faith Patterns," in J. Berryman (ed.), *Life Maps* (Waco: Winston Press, 1978), p. 64.

[41]   J. Moingt, "Laisser Dieu s'en aller," in J. Doré (ed.), *Dieu, Église, société* (Paris: Le Centurion, 1985), pp. 275–286.

Chapter Four

# Institutional Stage
# and Legalist Ethics

## Enlargement of the World

Despite his penchant for philosophical speculation, Lawrence Kohlberg was too rooted in the empirical methods of American psychosociology not to submit his theory to the ongoing process of experimental proof. He and his colleagues organized a "school within a school," called the *Cluster School,* in a secondary educational institution in Cambridge. In a "moral atmosphere of social justice" they were trying to educate youth according to Kohlberg's concept of development.[1]

[1]   L. Kohlberg, "Educating for a Just Society: An Updated and Revised Statement," in B. Munsey (ed.), *Moral Development, Moral Education, and Kohlberg: Basic Issues in Philosophy, Psychology, Religion, and Education* (Birmingham: Religious Education Press, 1980), pp. 455–470.

One of the most significant results of this educational experiment is the generalized incapacity of the students to go beyond a clannish conception of communal solidarity. The school has helped many girls and boys to move from an imperial and utilitarian view of human relations to a vision of interpersonal concord. Most of them, nonetheless, seem incapable of extending their loyalty beyond face-to-face relationships. To the degree that they identify their well–being with the "cause" of their tiny school, the students learn to recognize the immorality of lying and the failure to carry out their commitments within the structure of their school community. These views and interactions are not, however, effectively transferred to the larger society of which the *Cluster School* is merely a cell. The anonymity of the "lonely crowd" of the post–folkloric society[2] constitutes an insurmountable obstacle to a moral process that begins with a self mediated by the fusional.

Eventually girls and boys leave the warm greenhouse of secondary studies. This departure corresponds in general to one of the last steps towards the legal coming of age at 18, when they gain access to almost all the obligations and privileges of adulthood. Equipped with this new legal status the young adult enters either the work force or college. The second option does not, however, exclude the first since North American students usually work to help defray the astronomical costs of their college or university studies.

Even though a change of scene is never sufficient to provoke a new evolutionary movement, it often serves as its occasion. This is the case particularly at this stage just

---

[2]   D. Riesman, *The Lonely Crowd: A Study of the Changing American Character* (New Haven: Yale University Press, 1961).

as it was at the imperial stage when children left the family for school. Empirical research, whether in the Bahamas or Zambia, among the Inuit or kibbutzniks, shows that individuals living in villages in traditional sociocultural settings do not go beyond stage 3.[3] Obviously, even in Paris, New York or Montreal individuals can confine themselves to their neighbourhood or ghetto. Their experience of the human community is, then, similar to that of a Turkish or Amerindian villager.

Whatever the case, young people who set out one bright morning for work or college venture into a world that is larger than the culture of embeddedness that nourished their fusional adolescent identity. The familiar voices that defined the norms of action are drowned out by a cacophony that is difficult to decipher. Everyone around them has his or her own work and ideas. They expect newcomers to pull their own weight. The message these receive is clear, if not always subtle: "The success of your work and studies as well as how you conduct your private life is up to you alone. This isn't a nursery school."

William Perry has studied the effects of this radical change of environment on the lives of male students at Harvard and female students at Radcliff. He has carefully analysed how this has shaken their intellectual and moral development.[4] As Kegan emphasizes, this collegial experience of being thrown on their own is often resented and interpreted as "an abandonment, a refusal to care, and a

---

[3]    L. Kohlberg, C. Levine and A. Hewer, *Moral Stages* (Basel: S. Karger, 1983), p. 32.

[4]    W. G. Perry, Jr., *Forms of Intellectual and Ethical Development in the College Years* (New York: Rinehart and Winston, 1970), pp. 28–40.

disorienting vacuum of expectation."[5] The primordial question changes. In the community where he or she felt at home *(heimlichkeit)* the adolescent asked, "Who am I?"; in the impersonal, enlarged world of urban conglomerations, the young adult asks, "Who's in charge here?"

## Experiencing the Adult Order

The disequilibrium of the fusional truce that pushes an individual to leave the adolescent moratorium behind is caused, in my opinion, more by the demands of the social tasks that now arise than by the acquisition of a new cognitive tool or by the dynamics of psychic pressure. In all likelihood, in a society less complex than ours, the fusional solution functions well enough for the adult self. Perhaps further developments of the type we are describing are never needed or perhaps they progress along paths that empirical research cannot follow. It seems to me that there is no reason to hold this against Kohlberg.[6]

When he lays out the "seasons of a man's life" on the basis of a study of the development of 40 American males, Daniel Levinson no longer thinks of the adolescent moratorium as the springtime immediately preceding the summer of adult life. He describes the transition his subjects between 17 and 22 years of age make from adolescence to the threshold of the adult world. This passage levels out over

---

[5]    R. Kegan, *The Evolving Self* (Cambridge, Mass.: Harvard University Press, 1982), p. 186.

[6]    See the criticisms of E. L. Simpson, "Moral Development Research: A Case of Scientific Culture Bias," *Human Development,* Vol. 17, 1974, pp. 81–106; N. R. Haan, R. Weiss and V. Johnson, "The Role of Logic in Moral Reasoning and Development," *Developmental Psychology,* Vol. 18, 1982, pp. 245–256.

the next six years and comes to completion when the subjects are between 28 and 33 years of age.[7] That's how it works when development is successful. In a society as complex as our own, a large number of people never get beyond a stage 3 point of view. I repeat that, in the constructivist interpretation of the developmental sequence, we cannot predict the stage a subject has reached on the basis of age alone.

Normally, the impersonality and breadth of the adult order in our society pressures individuals into using a new style in their application of the formal cognitive operations. James Fowler calls this "dichotomizing."[8] Why? In their adult milieu, postadolescent individuals come to the realization that their clannish view of things is not self–evident. This confrontation between adolescent order and adult order pressures them into thinking in a hypothetical–deductive way so that they can more clearly differentiate themselves from others. In this world where pluralism makes itself felt for the first time, individuals reconsider their own points of view in the light of divergent outlooks. Their thinking becomes dichotomic. Linguistically this is expressed by alternative conjunctions: on the one hand . . . on the other/either . . . or.

This binary way of reasoning indicates that the cognitive structure has been modified. The conception that young adults have of the world has changed. The system that each one has constructed by an overly facile

---

[7]    D. Levinson, *The Seasons of a Man's Life* (New York: Ballantine, 1978), p. 71–135.

[8]    J. W. Fowler, "Life/Faith Patterns" in J. Berryman (ed.), *Life Maps* (Waco: Winston press, 1978), p. 71.

harmonization of the views of his or her peers and friends suffers the shock of being confronted by alien ideologies. They can no longer ignore them. At work they rub shoulders with bosses and colleagues who don't think the way they do at all. At the university level even the idea of "the truth" is given a death blow. Previously their teachers were content to transmit a specific content that others had already interpreted and systematized. Now those professors bright enough to initiate them into hermeneutics teach that there is more than one way to read a poem or interpret an historical event, an article of faith or a body of scientific data. In any area whatsoever, the division of knowledge into "truths" and "errors" is simplistic and inaccurate. Consequently, young people must work to reconstruct an ideology that will be more comprehensive and differentiated than what they had previously. Without this cognitive reconstruction, their success in the adult order is compromised.

In the dynamic of the ages of life, the structuration of intimacy which Erikson assigns to the young adult seems to characterize a more advanced period than we are presently discussing. Robert Kegan suggests that there is a stage missing in Erikson's theory between the industry age of late adolescence and the identity age towards the end of adolescence and the beginning of adulthood. He thinks we should insert the age of affiliation versus abandonment between these two ages of Erikson.[9] This suggestion has merit. However, one may also see Erikson's descriptions of the identity crisis as having two sides: the "crisis" side, describing the psycho-logical affinity of the adolescent self—

---

[9]     R. Kegan, *The Evolving Self*, p. 87.

in–conversation, and the "resolution" side, corresponding to psycho-logical independence. The evolutionary truce of the fourth stage is characterized by the second side.

## Institutional Self

Stage 4, like stage 2, indicates a return to the task of gaining independence. If the original identity of individuals remains immersed in intimate fusion, it will not be affirmed. The specific voice of each one will never be heard. With their own distinctive sound drowned out by the choir of familiar voices, they will be carriers of the common tune at best. If they want to come to adulthood they must, some day or other, take the floor and announce who they are. How will they come to make this gesture of authoritative empowerment that indicates a new sense of the self, self–independence and self–appropriation?

For Kegan, who sees the evolution of this meaning–making as a sort of spiral movement, the resolution of the adolescent identity crisis becomes possible when young adults move their relations with others, which have been, until now, part of their subjectivity, to the objective side of things. When they reach the point of objectifying them, they are able to see that they *are* not their relationships, they *have* them. "Having relationships" is something done by a subject distinct from others. It is by reflecting on the relationships they have, by co-ordinating them, and by situating themselves in relation to them that they give birth to the organizer–of–relationships self. Kegan calls this the "institutional" stage. The term evokes the psychic institution that the self who regulates social relationships has become.

In this respect the institutional self is like the imperial self — it restructures itself into a system. It is ready to deal satisfactorily with the multiplicity of social relationships encountered in the *conversatio civilis,* the interaction of civic life. After the self–in–conversation has spent time being assimilated to others, the pendulum of Piaget's movement of life adaptation points to a period of the self's accommodation.

For all that, however, the emotions and feelings that nourished the *conversatio amicalis* do not disappear. They are henceforth situated in the larger context of a psychic institution that constructs social roles and norms, and regulates the self. In a way, the objectivization of the "warm relations" with peers and friends allows these to be rediscovered and seen in a new light. The self is able to reappropriate them in terms of the respective place they hold in the adult order. The immediacy and the ultimate normativeness of fusional relationships with others have been replaced by organizational mediation. As Kegan says, the typical question is no longer, as at the preceding stage, "Do you still like me?" but "Does my government still stand?"[10]

We must be careful to interpret the relative independence of the institutional truce correctly. The self at stage 4 is an administrator, not a legislator. We are dealing with people whose meaning–making comes from the organization, not with people from whom the organization derives its own truth. Consequently, the self at stage 4 is still, inevitably, ideological. Nonetheless, a social ideology has replaced the narrow sectarian ideology of small, clannish communities with their overly restricted "causes."

---

[10]   Ibid., p. 102.

## Morality of the Social System

What are the moral implications of the new equilibrium the self has attained? The most important is that its conscience has become a social conscience. The good is what maintains the social system by correctly organizing civil relationships. Evil is what helps to overthrow this adult order. If, for example, you asked two stage 4 subjects about pornography, one might conclude that it is immoral because it disturbs the social order; the other might uphold the contrary position by arguing that it allows some men to relieve their sexual aggressivity by engaging in fantasy rather than in violent acts. The solutions are in opposition; the way of reasoning identical.

One does not have to score many Kohlbergian protocols to realize that the most characteristic answer of stage 4 subjects is "Tolerating such and such a way of acting would lead to social chaos." Because social chaos means the destruction of the basis of their institutional self–identity, it is seen as the diabolical representation of evil. Kohlberg long ago labelled stage 4 "the law and order stage." This fashionable expression perfectly portrayed the moral stance of the institutional self during the large scale social contestations that occurred throughout the western world in the sixties.

The new social conscience of stage 4 presupposes the construction of the moral notion of a right, a concept that did not even exist at the previous stage. Not that stage 3 subjects never discuss rights! The vocabulary morality uses does not change from one stage to the next. At whatever stage they are, people talk about good and evil, virtue and vice, law and norm, authority and freedom, conscience and responsiblity, justice and rights. However, at each stage this standard vocabulary is reconstructed from the ground up. Thus, for the fusional self, the notion of right is limited to the idea of "privilege," which the *Concise Oxford* defines as a "right, advantage or immunity, belonging to person, class or office; special advantage or benefit." This is exactly what "right" means to stage 3 individuals: the "private law" *(privi–legium)* of the group to which they belong. At stage 4, the enlargement of the notion of right is correlative to the size of the community to which they belong. Right becomes that which is demanded or permitted by conformity to a law that the society in which they hold membership recognizes as valid. It gives each individual control over a good (life, personal integrity, personal property, etc.); it puts others under obligation. Enriched by their rights and obligations, citizens enjoy a juridical existence regulated by a precisely determined measure of reciprocity.

The sense of justice of those at stage 4 follows the same trajectory as their notion of what a right is. At stage 3, justice means adopting the third party perspective internalized by the clan. At stage 4, justice means adopting the perspective of the generalized other. To decide what is just in social relationships, individuals can no longer refer simply to what those close to them think. Certainly stage 4 individuals continue to be influenced by these people, although they may not always be aware of it. However, they know that, when they are in conflict with others in society, the way to find a solution is to put themselves in their shoes, whoever they might be.

## The Primacy of Social Exigencies

At stage 3, the identity of individuals is so absorbed in the identity of the small defining groups that the self–in–conversation has, as yet, only a diffuse sense of its own identity. At stage 4, individuals confront this problem. The institutional truce indicates the first attempt to reconcile individual and social exigencies. The operation ends in favour of the common good. Individuals recognize the priority that social demands have over personal claims. From this point of view the psychologic of stage 4 independence is opposed to the psychologic of stage 2 independence. The first seeks an individualistic type of autonomy. The latter seeks individual autonomy through the mediation of a stable social order.

This evolutionary equilibrium proves itself superior to the preceding one. Armed with the morality of the social system, individuals take distance from the group. The institutional self now possesses moral rules to conduct its public life, and a private life that it did not have when it was at the fusional stage. This evolution indicates, moreover, a new degree of decentration. Even though they do not yet possess the key to judgment and moral decision, these moral subjects recognize a normative moral order of values. These no longer serve each individual watching out for his or her interest, as they did at the imperial stage, nor, as at the fusional stage, a small, privileged group keeping an eye on the interests of its own clannish cause. These values are normative for the whole of society. Individual and group goods are not excluded from moral considerations since the common good of society includes the good of each member. They do, however, have a subordinate rank in the hierarchy of goods. The transcendental character of the normative ethics has, then, made progress.

Even a summary exposition of a morality that gives priority to the social pole reveals its two major weaknesses. We note, first of all, the absence of a normative standard at the level of private life, which is regulated only inasmuch as some aspect of it has social implications. Kohlberg's reduction of the content of morality to the virtue and works of justice proves just how much conventional ideology is at the centre of his system. Justice, in fact, is the court of first instance regulating conflicts between persons functioning as actors on the social scene. Justice alone cannot shed light on judgments and moral choices related, for example, to veridicity (personal integrity) as distinct from veracity (the truthfulness due to others); on temperance in all its forms (sexual integrity, sobriety, frugality, etc.); or on courage and its various manifestations (audacity, active non–violent resistance, magnanimity, etc.). Thus, although the competent social authorities may dictate to us our moral obligations with respect to external acts that are likely to affect the juridical rights of others, they cannot legitimately deal with other external acts such as the expressions of friendship, liberality or authenticity, let alone interfere with the internal attitudes that inspire most of our moral activity. They can oblige us to pay our taxes; but they cannot make us do so out of love for distributive justice, patriotism or social fellowship.

The second flaw in this social morality is its lack of a critical base from which to criticize the morality of social ethics itself. How can we ensure that the social precepts are likely to promote our genuine common good? Does the legitimacy of social authority, whatever its political form, suffice to ensure that those who exercise it will always promulgate laws that will make us better human beings? Is the obedience given to lawful authority always a guarantee of morality? This was the major defence, remember, of the war criminals tried before an international military tribunal in Nuremberg between November 1945 and October 1946. The judges rejected this argument. They stated that, even in the absence of adequate international law, no authority can justify "crimes against humanity." Despite former U.S. president Richard Nixon's thoughts on the matter, what a chief of state does or says is neither automatically legal nor *a fortiori* moral.[11]

Calling up the special circumstances of Nazi Germany may make the danger of conventional morality seem something extraordinary. This illusion is dispelled by an experimental study conducted early in the sixties by Stanley Milgram.[12] Milgram wanted to measure how much physical punishment the "average American" was ready to inflict on another human being when someone in authority commanded him or her to do so. Milgram told his subjects that they were participating in a scientific experiment about learning techniques. Their task was to administer increasingly stronger electric shocks to another person for every wrong answer given. What Milgram's subjects actually heard was a tape recording of right and wrong answers, along with groans and cries after each electrical shock. The only factors keeping subjects from applying the maximum

---

[11]  D. Frost, *I Gave Them a Sword: Behind the Scenes of the Nixon Interviews* (New York: Ballantine, 1978).

[12]  S. Milgram, *Obedience to Authority* (New York: Harper & Row, 1974).

intensity was their compassion for the suffering individual
and their own moral judgment about the legitimacy of this
learning method. Contrary to all expectations, 65% of the
candidates obeyed Milgram's scientific authority right to
the end. In most cases, assuring the subjects that Yale University would assume responsibility for any bad consequences was enough to calm their scruples and hesitations.
What weight does a university professor's authority have
compared to Hitler's?

**Legalist Model**

In a chapter subtitled "Societal Ethics in Europe," Ver-
non Bourke sums up the thought of some twenty–five philosophers who, in the last three centuries, have maintained
"that a basis for ethical judgment is to be found in human
societies as they develop historically."[13] We do not, however, have to turn to philosophical writings for an ethical
model corresponding to stage 4 morality. The Judaeo–
Christian tradition has always sheltered a current of ethical
thought that thematizes moral experience around the symbol of the Law. Whether this law emanates ultimately from
a divine or human legislator has no effect on our proposal
since the identity of the legislator affects the ethical content
not the ethical form.

In the sixteenth century, the Dominican Bartholemew
de Medina gave the legalist model its first modern formulation in Catholic moral theology. This formulation was
immediately adopted by Jesuit moralists and systematized
as "probabilism." Blaise Pascal's attacks on the laxist de-

---

[13] V. J. Bourke, *History of Ethics* (Garden City: Doubleday, 1968),
pp. 219–234.

formations of this system are well known. Because of the excesses he condemned in his *Provinciales,* other systems were manufactured to compete with it. In the middle of the seventeenth century, the Dominican school challenged it with "probabiliorism."

In the eighteenth century, Alphonsus de Liguori, who had been trained in civil law, tried to reconcile these two systems in what is called "equiprobabilism." His work, which received Rome's support, succeeded in breaking the French clergy away from Jansenist rigorism, and went on to serve as a reference point for two centuries of confessors.[14] The legalist model has, then, profoundly marked our recent history. The fundamental positions of these systems using the legalist model can be elaborated in three points.[15]

First, in Plato's brief dialogue, "Euthyphron," Socrates asks, "Is what is holy holy because the gods approve it, or do they approve it because it is holy?"[16] If we translate that into the normative language of contemporary ethics, the Socratic question is equivalent to asking whether an action is commanded or forbidden because it is good or evil, or

---

[14]  On the work of Liguori, see Bernard Häring, *Free and Faithful in Christ: Moral Theology for Clergy and Laity* (New York: Seabury, 1978), Vol. 1, pp. 49–51; T. Rey–Mermet, *La morale selon saint Alphonse de Liguori* (Paris: Cerf, 1987).

[15]  F. L. Cross and E. A. Livingstone, "Probabilism," in *The Oxford Dictionary of the Christian Church* (London: Oxford University Press, 1974), pp. 1127–1128; J. Mahoney, *The Making of Moral Theology: A Study of the Roman Catholic Tradition* (Oxford: Clarendon Press, 1987), pp. 135–143.

[16]  Plato, "Euthyphron," 10a, E. Hamilton and H. Cairns (eds.), *The Collected Dialogues of Plato* (Princeton: Princeton University Press, 1961), p. 178.

whether it is good or evil because it is commanded or forbidden. Those following the probabilist model (I include all its emulators under this term) promptly answer that the commandment makes an action good and the interdiction makes it evil. In the beginning is the Law. The divine law orders cosmic confusion; the human law orders social chaos. This basic position makes probabilism an ethics, not of good and evil, but of the permitted and the forbidden.

What is the effect of this law? It directly attacks individual freedom by imposing a moral obligation on it. This is the second fundamental position. In probabilism the concept "freedom" takes on a juridical meaning. It is thought of as an innate right to use or abuse whatever is not forbidden by law. It is, therefore, something suspect, something linked to the egotism of the individual. In the subconscious of legalist moralists, liberty always suggests "libertinism". On the other hand, moral obligation always seems to encroach on the freedom of the individual because, until it is imposed by law, the individual has the right to act otherwise. The task of legalist ethics is, essentially, to verify the certainty or uncertainty of the obligations imposed by the law on individual freedom.

Who, then, will settle the debate? Conscience. This is the third fundamental position. What does probabilism mean by "conscience"? Conscience is thought of as a special faculty that plays the role of a court of justice within us. Before it the two parties of the litigation, Law and Freedom, present their respective witnesses and plead their case. After they have been heard the conscience weighs the plea for the defence and the charge of the prosecution according to a specific contentious procedure and pronounces the verdict. Probabilism and the systems that compete with it are distinguished from one another by the rules of procedure they advocate. The details of these contentious procedures are of less importance here than the nature of the juridical argumentation.

Moral subjects do not testify in their own defence. How could they? Only the legislator and his or her assistants exercise moral discernment. The question of determining whether or not a particular person in a specific situation may conceal such and such income in his or her tax return, break such and such an agreement, perform such and such a sexual act, or refuse such and such co-operation cannot be resolved by considering the human facts involved. To resolve these questions you have to consult the legislative texts to find out whether or not there is a law that authorizes or forbids such actions and you have to determine how it should be interpreted. How heavy is the obligation it imposes? What exactly does it stipulate? Does it apply to this particular case and in these particular circumstances? Does such and such an individual come under its jurisdiction? To resolve these questions and many others, the expertise of moralists–jurists is required.

In the court of conscience, the litigants mainly have recourse to the juridical opinions of professional casuists. If they all agree, the proceedings are brief. However, given the complexity of laws and circumstances, the experts are divided more often than not. Each system explains how the testimony of "authorized moralists," that is, those who are co-opted by the legal system in place, are to be weighed. A complex machinery of *imprimaturs,* recommendations, promotions or their opposites — censures, warnings and dismissals — make it possible to identify them. Thus, while the probabilist system favours freedom as long as an adequate though minority opinion can be put forward in its support, the probabiliorist system, on the contrary, favours the law and demands a clearly majority opinion before admitting the improbability of a moral obligation and, therefore, granting permission to "exercise one's freedom."

To be convinced of the juridical character of this science of moral standards, one need only verify the academic qualifications of the authors of the *Manuals of Moral Theology* published for the use of the Catholic clergy right up until the middle of the twentieth century. The great majority of them lay claim to a doctorate in canon and/or civil law. As civil servants in the employ of legalistic ethics, they specialized in the art of interpreting juridical texts.

## Consolidating Legal Norm

In favouring law as normative, the ethical model illustrated by probabilism rests on intuitions that no ethical reflection can afford to ignore. Each of its fundamental positions represents an acquisition of moral experience.

First, the existence and the importance of a law that assigns members their place in the whole and promotes their communal activity is a *sine qua non* for the moral existence of moral beings. An ethics that does not leave an important space for law is dysfunctional and not worth considering.

The second position concerning the rights of individual freedom also answers another primordial necessity of authentic moral existence: the structuration of the self in front of the forbidden. In a world where everything would give way before the desire of the individual, the self would never achieve the condition of an autonomous subject. A hundred years of psychoanalysis have made us acutely aware of the tasks of structuring desire by confronting it with the law.

Finally, by making conscience the faculty that weighs the opinions of the experts, the third position draws attention to a major fact of modern moral experience. To the degree that the complexity of our world increases, we are more and more aware of our personal limitations and the need we have of the competence of experts to help us get a better grasp of the facts of our moral dilemmas. Think of what is happening in biology, ecology and economics. Only the ignorant or the smug think they can dispense with competent advice in resolving all their moral dilemmas. Few people have acquired enough exact medical knowledge, for example, to evaluate correctly the advantages and disadvantages of such and such a surgical procedure. Everyday, however, thousands of serious, conscientious people all over the world make the serious moral decision, on the advice of their doctors, to risk their lives on the operating table.

The emergence of the law as a norm in the moral lives of individuals consolidates their social identity as well as their moral stance. They no longer go begging for their identity and their rules of conduct in five or six discordant communities. The social institution, with its conventional definitions, norms and experts, offers a frame which allows them to put their lives in order and confidently to begin the work of being adults.

## Moral Objectivism

The foundational positions of legalist ethics are, none-theless, subject to criticism: less in themselves than in terms of the place they hold in the whole picture and, con-sequently, in terms of the significance that they assume.

Legal meaning–making ultimately consists in assign-ing the social system responsibility for fixing the bounda-ries of individual desires according to the common good. Moral obligation, therefore, only reaches the individual as an external force. Individuals do not discover any deep complicity in their own internal resources with those things that are permitted or any visceral repugnance to those things that are forbidden. They themselves do not possess the means to recognize the specific validity of every moral obligation imposed by the law. The legal obligation is nei-ther perceived nor felt as answering a personal aspiration towards the good which predates the social code and its ex-ternal guarantee of social security. Therefore, the moral work done by precept is never an "original." The individual could not sign his or her name to it without committing fraud. One neither signs nor dedicates a photocopy. The subjectivity necessary to moral creation is lacking.

Like criminal law, legalist ethics is busy setting the limits for freedom's exercise. Should we be astonished then to discover here nothing more than a morality of sin that fosters a perpetual anguish in the moral agent: "Have I or have I not violated the frontier separating what is allowed from what is sin . . . slight sin from serious sin?" In return, legalist ethics offers a good conscience. The effort to obey the law and all the legal rituals that support it appease the sense of guilt that constantly surfaces in all those who count on a legal system for their moral salvation.

Moral objectivism considerably reduces the personal sense of good and evil. Virtue and vice boil down to obedience and disobedience to the social order. Whether they attribute a divine or human origin to this makes no difference. Respecting others or despising them, bravely resisting injustice or cowardly fleeing it, using the limited resources of our planet with moderation or squandering them are not acts whose specific goodness or evil is recognized in themselves. If the authority of the divine or human legislator does not decree them good or evil, they are morally indifferent.

According to Kohlberg, only 25% of the population of the United States reaches the fifth stage of moral development.[17] Is it surprising then to learn that, according to periodic opinion polls, a large majority of Americans deny rights to their fellow citizens which, though the respondents are unaware of it, are guaranteed by the American Bill of Rights?[18] Only individuals who have surpassed the conventional level of morality can appreciate the profound aspirations of our humanity that lie beyond legal determinations.

---

[17]   L. Kohlberg and E. Turiel, "Moral Development and Moral Education" in G. L. Lesser (ed.), *Psychology and Educational Practice* (Glenview: Scott and Foresman, 1971), pp. 410–465.

[18]   D. Yankelovich, *Generation Apart* (New York: Columbia Broadcasting System, 1969).

## Religious Institutionalism and the Legislator God

Of all the ethical models, the legal model is the one that has the most predictable consequences for religion and faith. Necessarily organized according to one or another historical model of society, the major churches, especially, offer their faithful an obvious religious version of a legal meaning–making of existence. Though the religious purism of the loyalist model has not disappeared from the religious horizon of conventional subjects at stage 4, it cedes its place to the institutionalism that is characteristic of the major modern churches.

The sects correspond to the viewpoint and needs of those who can only function well when they are identified with restricted religious groups that can define clearly delimited causes (these are often moral issues): for life and against abortion, for ecology and against acid rain, for peace and against nuclear armament, for decency and against pornography. These sects lay out delimited dogmas and codes of conduct in formulas that are both intellectually simplistic and emotionally charged.

Individuals who have gone on to the next landing of the evolution of meaning–making can no longer tolerate sectarian discourse. Even when they belong to a major church, they find whatever is sectarian in its religious and moral discourse intolerably suffocating. If these individuals continue to value their church, it is, on the contrary, because of its "catholicity" (its universality), the latitude of individual freedom and the collective security offered by its tradition and its imposing hierarchical organization. When they continue to belong to a church, the partisans of a legalist ethics are best served by the large, highly institutionalized churches of which the Roman Catholic Church remains the prototype in the western world.

If the faithful do not have a very good grasp of what the dogmas and theological traditions of their church contain, they do know about their existence and secular prestige. They are confident that, in their church, among its hierarchy and its intelligentsia, there are men and, more recently, women who know divine revelation and how to defend and explain it. The faithful with an institutional self know where to knock when they need to know what they should think or do. Every time parliament is busy with a bill that has complex moral considerations, bishops and theologians are asked by their co-religionists in government and by the media for clarification of "the exact position of the Church." Since the institutional organization is complex and diversified, each person retains the initiative to select at least his or her own religious spokesperson and his or her director of conscience.

Whether the partisans of legalistic ethics call the divinity "Father," "Good Shepherd" or "Lord," God is always thought of as the Legislator. The images of Yahweh dictating the commandments to Moses on Sinai, or of Jesus vested as "Christ the King," express well the God behind the formulas that the faith of believers at this stage reaches. This "Master of the Universe," to use the popular talmudic expression, may be an object of veneration or even of authentic love. His "numinous" mystery runs the risk, however, of frightening *(tremendum)* more than it attracts *(fascinans)*.[19] Faith at this stage is characterized more by

---

[19] R. Otto, *The Idea of the Holy* (Oxford: Oxford University Press, 1929).

ignorance before what this mystery can evoke of the hidden and obscure than by the surplus of knowledge that those who share in the warm light of the divine *logos* enjoy.

Chapter Five

# Interindividual Stage
# and
# Humanist Ethics

## Crisis of Institutionalism

Each developmental evolutionary truce falls apart when the very solutions it makes temporarily possible are called into question. Thus, for subjects at stage 4, it is precisely the institutional style of the relationship between the individual and society that becomes the target of their dissatisfaction and criticism. It is precisely the social experience of adults that puts the institutional solution in question.

Except in extremely stable and harmonious social circumstances, everyone who shares in adult life is forced to realize, sooner or later, that institutions and those who direct them are fragile. The political systems to which individuals belong give rise to instances of flagrant injustice and allow ecological disasters of incalculable magnitude. The companies for which they work put the profit of share-holders before the interests of their customers, employees or the environment. The churches in which they worship preach respect for rights they do not respect in their own organizations. There is no institution where those in charge do not contravene the norms that they have the mandate to uphold. Some politicians and some government bureau-crats are accused of "legal" fiscal frauds or embezzlement. Some pastors who take a rigorist line are charged with sex-ual abuse by women and minors. Some parents who are stalwart defenders of "traditional family values" make fam-ily life intolerable for their children.

The majority of adults who confront these social facts come to terms with them. "What do you expect," they say, "people are weak! Then too, all things considered, it is bet-ter to have the democracy of the free world (the universal-ity of the Catholic church, the security of marriage, or whatever) despite its limitations and failings than the slav-ery of communism (the sectarianism of Protestantism, the licentiousness of the unmarried, and so on)." Of all moral theories, that of the lesser evil is the most popular in the adult world. In this world, virtually every organization cul-tivates the uncontested acceptance of the institutional *sta-tus quo*. Even organizations concerned with knowledge and values tend to suffer from this common organizational syn-drome which prompts them to make their own continuance, rather than the promotion of the ideals on which they were founded, their *raison d'être*.[1]

---

[1]     See W. Torbert, *Creating a Community of Inquiry: Conflict, Col-laboration, Transformation* (New York: Wiley, 1976).

A certain number of people are dissatisfied with this solution. It does not adequately regulate what the institutional truce claims to establish: an equilibrium in the relationship between the individual and society. A society that resolves its survival problems to the detriment of its members, or of some of them, is no longer exercising the harmonizing function that the subjects assigned it. The organizational form that the self took on unveils its tyrannical face. It blocks the development of the subjects. Perhaps the polarization of the public and the private is itself simply a function of the evolutionary equilibrium of stage 4! Doesn't it create more problems than it solves?

If adults are actively involved in the institutions to which they belong, they themselves attain to posts of authority and influence. The junior executives become partners with places on the administrative council. As young adults they received a great deal, as Daniel Levinson shows, from their relationship with a mentor. Today, their young colleagues choose them as mentors.[2] They have moved from being spouses to being parents. They are called to exercise towards their children and towards their junior partners the seventh task of Erikson's adult age: "generativity." This is not a matter of accidentally bringing children into the world. Psychodynamically it means the concern to establish and guide the younger generation. Without the virtue of care, which sustains and feeds this effort, adults develop a pervasive sense of stagnation.

---

[2]    D. J. Levinson, *The Seasons of a Man's Life* (New York: Ballantine, 1978), pp. 97–101 and 333–335.

The institutional equilibrium has structured an organization to order and control the relationships of the subject. A new equilibrium is beginning to structure a self capable of running the organization.

## Meta–ethical Questioning

As we saw in the introductory chapter, the reinterpretation of the Kohlbergian sequence which prolongs moral development beyond adolescence was partly due to the discovery, at the beginning of the seventies, of protocols that Kohlberg decided to score 4 1/2. He was dealing with protocols produced by people who, though they had earlier shown the capacity to make moral judgments at stage 4, seemed suddenly to regress towards the relativism of stage 2. When he examined these protocols more closely, he realized that he was not dealing with the utilitarian sort of relativism. After facing the failure of the stage 4 institutional solution, these subjects demonstrated a cultural relativism. Attached as he was to Piaget's conception of thought as a logical function, Kohlberg was unable to understand correctly the new meta–ethical questioning of the subject whose protocols were scored at stage 4 1/2.[3]

The reflections of these subjects had less to do with the form of moral norms than with preliminary questions concerning the nature and specificity of the human being, the meaning of values and personal commitment, and the cultural contextuality of moral discernment. These ques-

---

3    A. Guindon, "Moral Development. Form, Content, and Self: A Critique of Kohlberg's Sequence," *University of Ottawa Quarterly*, Vol. 48, 1978, pp. 232–263.

tions arise from what we today call meta–ethics. Why this new mode of questioning?

The social experience of the adults we have just described launches a real intellectual revolution in minds that are somewhat astute. The classics of literature offer a number of famous versions of the "crisis" of meta–ethical questioning: William Shakespeare's Hamlet, Fedor Dostoevski's Raskolnikov, James Joyce's Stephen Daedalus. Erik Erikson has studied many historical cases in his work: Luther, Darwin, Jefferson, Freud and Gandhi. Although the questions of all those who critically consider the institutional equilibrium may be less well-known, they likewise change levels: it is no longer a matter of "to act or not to act" but "to be or not to be."

That is the question! James Fowler has clearly shown that his stage 5 subjects are no longer satisfied, as they were at the preceding stage, to interpret symbols as precise and univocal concepts. They begin to perceive what symbols really are. They grasp their partiality, relativity, ambiguity and their evocative value. Consequently, they progress to a demythologization of both linguistic and social symbols. At the beginning of the crisis, they are tempted to conclude that the whole business is arbitrary, relative to each culture, even to each individual. Truth/ falseness, goodness/malice, masculinity/femininity or kinship/filiation are only cultural fabrications. With an intolerance of which they are unaware, they preach tolerance towards what seems to them to be merely different points of view that are all equally legitimate. Kegan insightfully remarks that this stage 4 1/2 position "confuses the idea that all persons are entitled to hold whatever beliefs they wish with a second idea, that there is no non-arbitrary basis upon which to compare these beliefs."[4]

The adult intellectual crisis ends with the realization that, though systems of thought, values and interaction are constructed by thinking, value–creating and interacting subjects, this does not mean that these systems should not be compared to one another nor evaluated in relation to one another. The result is a new way of thinking which, as Fowler notes, becomes dialectical.[5] It is open to paradox, the multiplicity of systems, the plurality of models of coherence. Instead of hardening the opposition between paradoxical positions to come to a choice of one against the other, it prefers to consider the interrelation of the poles in order to take hold of the more inclusive movements, processes and organizational contexts. Behind the different interacting social groups, for example, it perceives the human community to which they all belong. The more it consolidates thoughts, values and personal choices the more easily it finds a place in life for a bit of ambiguity, mystery and wonder, the *thauma* that Aristotle made the source of all philosophical thinking.[6] We can understand why Fowler named stage 5, the "paradoxical–consolidative" stage.

## Interindividual Self

In her book, *Passages*, Gail Sheehy writes that "somewhere between the late thirties and early forties when we

---

4     R. Kegan, *The Evolving Self* (Cambridge: Harvard University Press, 1982), p. 66.

5     On this idea, see M. Basseches, *Dialectical Thinking and Adult Development* (Norwood: Ablex, 1984).

6     Aristotle, *Metaphysics*, I, 2 (982 b 11–21; 983 a 12–20).

enter midlife, we also have the opportunity for true adult-hood, whereupon we proceed either to wither inside our husks or to regather and re–pot ourselves for the flowering into our full authenticity."[7] Is there not a turning back on oneself in both cases? Not at all! That is what distinguishes the individualism of stage 2 from the interindividuality of stage 5.

Psychodynamically, the crisis of the institutional struc-ture of the self places it in a no man's land. The loss of institutional absolutes is just as uncomfortable psychologi-cally as it is intellectually. In Gail Sheehy's work, we hear the men and women she interviewed confess to the internal upheaval they experienced when the social roles on which they had depended, and which they played to the best of their ability, no longer answered their pressing internal summons. In his study of the emotional stages of life, Sam Keen was so impressed by the upheaval aspect of the de-struction of the *persona* of the interiorly well–ordered sub-ject, its myths, conventions, masks, roles,and defences, that he named the subject at this stage "the outlaw self." Ac-cording to Keen, the virtue of conversion *(metanoia)* char-acterizes this stage.[8]

In his own evolutive scheme of nine stages, following the relativist position, William Perry describes a position which he labels "commitment foreseen." Since he thinks that human development is not merely a matter of cognitive evolution but implies ego strength, he invokes three

---

[7]     G. Sheehy, *Passages: Predictable Crises of Adult Life* (New York: Bantam Books, 1977), p. 49.

[8]     S. Keen, *The Passionate Life* (New York: Harper and Row, 1983), pp. 128–186.

foreseeable scenarios.[9] Anticipating the choices that will
have to be made and the responsibility they bear for these
choices and for acting on them, individuals can refuse to go
any further and can regress towards ideological positions
assumed earlier. They barter their freedom for institutional
security, sometimes even for neurosis.[10] Instead of resolving the crisis negatively, as in the preceding scenario, others stall and settle nothing. If they prolong their stay in
cynicism's refuge, it is not a good omen for their psychological equilibrium. The positive scenario opens onto Perry's next position, a specific initial involvement in
authentically intimate relationships.[11]

One could argue that at stage 4 we are dealing with
adults who are already involved in the work world and, often, have conjugal and parental responsibilities as well.
That's true. George Vaillant's study of adult development
shows, however, that current definitions of intimacy, in
terms of the number of years married to the same person, or
a cultural assortment of behaviour patterns, are false. Alliances that have lasted for many years may not only lack real
intimacy but also support a partner's resistance to any evolution that might make intimacy possible.[12]

---

[9]   W. J. Perry, Jr., *Forms of Intellectual and Ethical Development
in the College Years* (New York:: Rinehard and Winston, 1970), pp. 134-
152.

[10]   See the case of Dora, the only girl whose neurosis Freud analysed
in his work:  S. Freud,"Fragmen of Analysis of a Case of Hysteria," in J.
Strachey (ed.), *The Standard Edition of the Complete Psychological
Works of Sigmund Freud* (London: The Hogarth Press and the Institute of
Psycho-analysis, 1953-1966), vol. VII, pp. 3-122.

[11]   W. J. Perry, *Forms of Intellectual and Ethical Development in the
College Years*. pp. 149–158.

Intimacy which allows individuals to enter into communion from deep within themselves is the product of selves who manage to distinguish themselves from social organizations. Instead of defining them as subjects, these organizations now pass over to the objective side of things. The new selves can finally discover themselves in their proper individual consistency. Instead of *being* their duties, roles and social systems, they *have* them. They regulate them by their own sense of interdependence with others who are both so like them in their humanity and so distinct from them in their individuality. The collapse of the institutional equilibrium disposes individuals towards an intimate sharing of an altogether different scope than the fusional efforts of stage 3. The new form of reciprocity "now becomes a matter of at once mutually preserving the other's distinctness while interdependently fashioning a bigger context in which these separate identities interpenetrate, by which the separate identities are co-regulated, and to which persons invest an affection supervening their separate identities."[13]

The new evolutionary truce of the interindividual self is as much the consequence as the cause of intimate experience. Under the generous regard of those who love them for themselves, individuals learn to esteem their own worth. Thus they give birth to themselves. They discover their real aspirations, not those that have been imposed on them; their real likes and dislikes, not those they were told they should have; their real talents, not those others wanted them to acquire; their real absolutes, not those others

---

[12]  G. E. Vaillant, *Adaptation to Life* (Boston: Little, Brown, 1977).
[13]  R. Kegan, *The Evolving Self*, p. 253.

wanted them to adopt. Does the task of "intimacy," which is opposed to the isolation Erikson assigns to the sixth age, really precede the generativity of the seventh age, or is it its fruit? One wonders. In order for this virtue of love, which characterizes the successful fulfilment of the task of intimacy, to flourish, the partners must reciprocally receive the other's care.

## Morality of the Social Contract

While the social, cognitive and psychodynamic tasks are being completed, the form of moral judgment changes. It not only changes stages, Kohlberg thinks, but also levels. After the normativity of the fusional and then the social expectations of conventional morality, the subjects now count on the discernments to which they come on their own.

Since Kohlberg reduces the content of morality to the area of justice, he labels stage 5 a social contract morality. In his mind this expression has a different meaning than the "morality of the social system" at stage 4. At stage 5, in effect, social rules are no longer seen as the product of the social system. They are understood to result from a "social contract" signed by adults who come to agreement about the rational validity of the social rules that *they themselves* make. All who fulfil the social obligations they consider to be based on universally accepted principles act well. The authentic moral and legal obligations of justice can only be discerned in a "prior to society" perspective, that is, a perspective that takes the common humanity of all persons, regardless of what community they belong to, as its base.

The transitory crisis of the relativist morality of stage 4 1/2 is definitely resolved by the discovery that, the limits and injustices of the social system notwithstanding, a rational human basis transcends these historical factors. The construction of principles that can be universalized permits the identification of a moral source anterior to the authority of the groups promulgating the rules of positive law. Under Kant's formulations we can recognize the old idea, as Kohlberg often pointed out, of a "natural law" which is the basis of all human law. Stage 5 moral agents localize their deontological activity (which puts forward moral duties) in a context that is anterior to the existence of concrete social systems.

Since 1971 Kohlberg has made the scenario described by philosopher John Rawls his own.[14] According to Rawls, the ideal of justice could be achieved by fully rational persons who, before the establishment of any social constitution, would weigh the rights and duties of each individual. This original activity would unfold under "the veil of ignorance": each founding person would be ignorant of the cultural circumstances of the society coming to birth, of the place that he or she occupied in it, and of the roles and functions he or she exercised within it.The only principles these individuals would have would be those they could rationally deduce through their common humanity thirsting for fairness.

---

[14]    J. Rawls, *A Theory of Justice* (Cambridge: Harvard University Press, 1971).

## Discovery of Human Dignity

Since the postconventional level implies a meta–ethical questioning, the philosophical thought of the researchers has greater influence on their hermeneutics than at the preconventional and conventional levels. Consequently, the discussion of the interpretation of the data is more heated than elsewhere. It is not easy to distinguish the moral ideas of stage 5 subjects from those of Kohlberg or any other researcher.

The majority of researchers would probably agree that at this evolutionary stage of ethical meaning–making there is an existential disclosure that is decisive for the quality of judgment and moral commitment — the discovery of "human dignity." Regardless of the interpretation that they might give it, they generally acknowledge that at the inter-individual stage this factor becomes ethically normative.

Moral subjects at the postconventional level obey only the rules they impose on themselves. It's not that they reject the normativity of laws and rules set down and promulgated by others; rather, as much as possible, they submit every rule of conduct to their own critical discernment before considering themselves morally bound by it. Acts are not good or evil because they are permitted or forbidden; they become prescriptive or interdictive when they are judged good or evil. Why? Because moral rules only command respect and a sense of obligation to the degree that their humanizing value is evident to right reason. The ultimate basis of moral existence has become the person in his or her human dignity. They conclude that they are obliged to achieve whatever favours this human quality in themselves and others, and to avoid whatever brings this eminent dignity under attack.

This new norm marks an advanced phase in the process of moral transcendence. Humanity represents a more universal norm than the law of this state or that church. It leaves no room for exclusivism and certainly not for any legislative arbitrariness. All legislation and all legislators are carefully screened in terms of the demands of human dignity. Any precept, whether of human or supposedly divine origin, that can be shown to be dehumanizing is not an authentic law but, as the scholastics used to say, "a corruption of the law."

We must also take into account that the normativity of human dignity opens every human act, whether in the social or private sphere, to moral discernment. Their reduction of morality to justice has prevented Kohlberg and his colleagues from understanding this point. As we have seen, so long as the ultimate norm remains a positive form of the law (or a "natural law" actually conceived on the model of a "positive law" promulgated by God and interpreted by ecclesiastical authority), a vast area of human conduct necessarily escapes moral examination. Nothing slips by the norm of the human. It does not need to be promulgated officially by someone before it imposes itself on the conscience of moral subjects. Not only all law but the whole self comes under the jurisdiction of "the human."

The Platonic intellectualism avowed by Kohlberg imposes on postconventional morality another restrictive interpretation which creates unnecessary difficulties. Since his morality is quartered in the cognitive area, his stage 5 subjects look like yogis. They are content to proclaim human meaning–making instead of planning, like responsible agents, creative actions of humanizing meaning–making. Morality, however, is less a science than an art. We do not qualify as "moral" those who talk on and on, but never act. [15] Once the human meaning of a situation has been drawn out, this meaning has to be embodied in actions which promote human dignity. The Kohlbergian style of ethics of conviction have to be completed by an ethics of responsibility. [16]

## Humanist Model

When I qualify the ethical model which seems to correspond to stage 5 as "humanist," I have no intention of distinguishing it from either an "illiterate" or a "deistic" model. The term should be understood in its proper sense. A "humanist" model is one in which human dignity is the ultimate norm. Thus, a Christian philosopher as influenced by theology as Jacques Maritain could still label his philosophical system an "integral humanism." [17]

The systems within the humanist model come in all colours. Since this book fits into the global project of Christian reflection, I shall illustrate this humanist model by the system which has exercised a lasting influence on moral theology in the Catholic Church, even if it has never been adopted by the mass of believers for reasons that moral development research makes evident. This system is that

---

[15] Aristotle, *Nicomachean Ethics*, II, 3 (1105 b 10–15).

[16] A. Guindon, "Kohlberg's Postconventional Yogis," *Église et Théologie*, Vol. 12, 1981, pp. 279–306.

[17] J. Maritain, *Integral Humanism: Temporal and Spiritual Problems of a New Christendom* (New York: C. Scribner's Sons, 1968).

which Thomas Aquinas perfected in the second part of his *Summa Theologiae*. Since his ethical thought is more refined and differentiated than that which is at work in probabilism, readers are asked to be indulgent towards the author's presentation "in three points." The majority of those who study the *Summa* agree, I believe, that in the ethics of Thomas Aquinas the following three positions are fundamental: the primacy of the end, prudential discernment, and the virtuous improvement of the moral agent.

By thematizing moral experience around the notion of obligation imposed by the external law, legalist morality fits Henri Bergson's conception of a "closed morality": a morality of social pressure, retention, attachment to tradition and conformity.[18] Thomas, on the contrary, thematizes moral experience around the notion of aspiration towards being. An "open morality" in Bergson's terminology, a morality of desire, progress, oriented towards the future and human renewal. At the beginning is "the fullness of being" which seduces, draws and summons us to participation and to sharing with others. The moral project is designed in view of the goal of human existence and in the loving desire to engender it in the self in interaction with others. Consequently, Thomas opens his ethical discourse with a formal philosophical reflection on the last end. This is what structures all of moral existence.[19] Since he is a theologian, he interprets the content of this end in terms of Beatitude. Created in the image of God,[20] the human creature is called

---

[18]    H. Bergson, *The Two Sources of Morality and Religion* (New York: Doubleday, Anchor, 1954).

[19]    Thomas Aquinas, *Summa Theologiae*, Ia–IIae, Q. 1 to 4.

[20]    *Ibid.*, Prologue to second part.

by grace to share the very life of God revealed in Jesus Christ.[21]

When individuals are old enough to take charge of their own lives, they enter into the adult moral order by thinking about themselves in terms of the ultimate end. By posing this "fundamental option," they initiate the existential project of the human communion to which God has graciously given Covenant value.[22] The introspection of the legalist model has given way to a morality that today is labelled prospective. The deontological (the logic of obligation: *deon*) approach began by laying down the means: "Do what you should." The teleological approach (the logic of the end: *telos*) begins by inviting people to pursue the humanizing goal: "Become what you are." This is the job that all men and women have in common.

If the fundamental option for an end which structures the horizon of desire and meaning–making is logically first in the Thomist conception of moral life, the effective realization of the desire to be is not at all neglected. In a Montreal lecture some time ago, Paul Ricoeur recalled that the whole moral pattern comes to birth in this gap between what we profoundly desire and our real life. For the finite and historical beings we are, the problem of the gap is more complex than it appears. First, the good only shows itself to us refracted through a multitude of particular values. The choices we must make never come forward in the general form of good or evil. They appear as justice or injustice, truth or falsehood, courage or cowardice. Gradually, each

---

21  *Ibid.*, Ia–IIae, Q. 1 to 5.
22  *Ibid.*, Q. 89, art. 6.

one of us must proceed, in interaction with others, towards a clarification and a hierarchization of his or her values.

The task of actualization does not stop there. Human life is more concrete than this first scenario suggests. Our moral dilemmas are never restricted to a theoretical choice for justice versus injustice or for moderation versus excess. Who isn't for justice? The moral challenge is to be effectively committed to an action that can promote justice in the concrete circumstances of our life. Individuals should, then, dedicate themselves to the daily task of freely exercising their reason, under the loving influence of the ultimate end and the moral values which refract it so as to discern and choose the means for its humane and humanizing insertion in the world. This process of prudential judgment represents the second fundamental position of the Thomist system.[23]

The obligation that results from this discernment of practical wisdom *(prudentia)* does not have the absolute form of the legalist *diktat*. In the Thomistic conception, it makes no sense to speak of "absolute obligations." Moral obligation always has a conditional form: it is conditioned by the nature of the bond which agents establish between the acquisition of the humanizing end they desire and the utilization of the means they discern.[24]

Compared to probabilism, then, the original Thomism puts being before the law and prudential discernment before the weight of the opinions of others in the tribunal of conscience. The original Thomism also differs

---

[23]   *Ibid.*, IIa–IIae, Q. 46–47.

[24]   J. Tonneau, *Absolu et obligation en morale* (Paris: Vrin, 1965).

fundamentally from the legalist system in a third way. It puts the person of the moral agent before his or her acts. Consequently, the study of the virtues becomes the major part of moral consideration. This study is missing from the works of probabilist moralists. All attention is centred on forbidden and permitted acts. If they get around to talking about "virtuous" or "vicious" acts, they mean nothing more by these adjectives than "permitted" and "forbidden."

In Thomistic ethics, on the contrary, "virtue" means an entitative enrichment of the agents and, consequently, a new "virtuosity" in the elaboration of actions that enrich themselves and the human community. The order of priorities is reversed. At the conclusion of their trajectory, neither the agents nor anyone else is interested in knowing how many good acts have been listed to their credit. The quality of their being and their presence, not the number of their transactions, makes people appealing and worthy of being loved. It is no different in the evening of life. People who have become as good as their end, who have fully brought themselves to birth, have completed their fundamental task of humanization. The dignity of the human person is ultimately normative.[25]

## Moral Mastery

The principal merit of the humanist model is that it makes moral agents "masters of their own houses." By making humanization the end, the cornerstone, the model

---

[25] On this notion of virtue, see S. Pinckaers, "Virtue Is Not a Habit," in *Cross Currents*, Vol. 12, 1962, pp. 65–81; G. C. Meilaender, Jr., *The Theory and Practice of Virtue* (Notre Dame: Notre Dame Press, 1984), pp. 18–44.

offers individuals the key to the moral project. They do not have to beg superior beings for its meaning. By interacting with their fellow human beings, they can make sense of their moral journey, both that part they share with others and that part which is theirs alone. Their moral life no longer seems fragmented, and made up of separate pieces that others hand them to meet needs as they arise along the way. An overall intentionality unifies the values of human existence and links commitments to one another. Although acts of obedience can play a role in serving the common good, this virtue and its actions do not come close to exhausting the richness of the moral life. Nor does obedience furnish the global meaning–making of the moral life nor assure the interconnection of the virtues.[26]

This mastery also gives the humanist model a dynamic aspect lacking in the preceding model where the system regulates the decision to be made. Because the moral implementation of existence is done under the impulse of a cognitive and affective orientation, it takes the form of an inventive process. The responses to moral dilemmas are never thought of as prefabricated; they have to be created right in the situations by the agents themselves. They will call on the resources that are available, including, of course, legal stipulations, the opinions of experts, and "friendly pieces of advice." The main sources of the decision, however, remain the foundational certitudes and the connaturality with the good that long practice of the fundamental option has developed in the agents. Virtuous mastery represents their capacity to respond spontaneously,

---

[26] Thomas Aquinas, *Summa Theologiae*, Ia–IIae, Q. 65.

coherently and easily. [27] Human beings who are enlightened interiorly by an end that is known and desired, and whose own deliberations invent their actions are freed from the crushing weight of external constraints. Freedom, the Second Vatican Council said, is

> an exceptional sign of the divine image within man. For God has willed that man be left "in the hand of his own counsel" (Sirach 15:14) so that he can seek his Creator spontaneously, and come freely to utter and blissful perfection through loyalty to Him. Hence man's dignity demands that he act according to a knowing and free choice. Such a choice is personally motivated and prompted from within. It does not result from blind internal impulse nor from mere external pressure. [28]

Only in freedom do individuals shed the labels given them by their families, defining groups and society. These labels keep them from discovering their real personality and actualizing their full potential.

## Rationalism

Even in its best versions, such as the Thomism of Thomas Aquinas, the humanist ethical model cannot escape the charge of a certain rationalism. I want to point out some of its aspects.

This rationalism is already evident in the first fundamental position. The idea that, when the time comes, individuals deliberate about their total selves and opt for "an end" that will guide them until the end of their days, gives human reason what is perhaps superhuman power. Whether or not it is illumined by religious faith, human reason is

---

[27]  Thomas Aquinas, *Disputed Questions: The Virtues*, Q. 1, art. 1.

[28]  Pastoral Constitution, *The Church in the Modern World*, No. 17.

considered capable, at an earthly stage of its development, of grasping the global intelligibility of life and putting it into action.

Certain specific traits change in astute people as they grow older. But is there not reason to fear that a moral project, elaborated on the basis of an initial Dream, contains an idealization that will necessarily prove inadequate and deceptive in the future? Will individuals, striving towards an ideal conceived at this or that age or in this or that circumstance, be attentive to the real direction of their human becoming? Will the signs that their bodies, their emotions, their desires, those around them and their new circumstances transmit to them really be picked up and decoded? Will they provide an opportunity thoroughly to rethink their orientation? Are they not more likely, on the contrary, to seem like accusations of infidelity to the ideal? By according human reason the power to grasp the meaning of history before it unfolds, humanist ethics involves a perfectionism that is a script for self–defeat and self–blame. A feeling of defeat lies in wait for travellers on a route marked out by reason before the intervention of the vicissitudes of human freedom and the hazards of the journey.

The priority accorded to reason in the prudential discernment of the means is also marred by a blissfully optimistic rationalism. This defect is present even in the interpretation which specifies that moral discernment must be "right," that is, that reason must be rectified by an authentic love of the end. The heart has its own reasons, and reason probably knows less about them than those who acknowledge the truth of the Pascalian aphorism are willing to admit. They could go on asking indefinitely why it is that, when the moral judgment has come to a halt, the agent decides to act or not to act, or to act this way instead of that way. They may never find out, because the pull that ultimately engenders the act no longer belongs to reason but to the mysterious domain of the "heart."

By giving priority to the virtuous improvement of individuals, Thomistic ethics lends itself to an individualistic conception of the moral project, even if this deviation is perhaps not congenital to it. All individuals, equipped as they are with reason which reflects on the inclinations of their heart and promulgates "natural laws" from it, are ultimately responsible in their soul and conscience to make their own decisions about the good and evil of their acts.[29] All individuals examine the ways of human nature within themselves, set out the laws and dictate their concrete applications. Perhaps, despite what legend tells us, Thomas Aquinas, who died towards the end of the fourth decade of his life, did not have enough existential experience of the "vanity of vanities" of Qoheleth, the sage of Israel.

## Religious Intellectualism and the Divine Logos

The humanist model of the moral life predisposes religious individuals to reconstruct the universe of faith quite differently. The faith is finally ready to devote itself to what an ancient tradition understood theology to be: *fides quaerens intellectum,* faith seeking to make sense of itself. Faith is no longer seen as absence of knowledge, confession of ignorance and blind obedience to the mediators chosen by God to resolve our human perplexities. On the contrary, faith becomes clairvoyant. It is to terrestrial trav-

---

[29]   Thomas Aquinas, *Summa Theologiae*, Ia–IIae, Q. 19, art. 5 and 6.

ellers what vision is to the blessed. A still imperfect participation in the divine light, it renders the daughters and sons of God capable of giving a Christian reading of the events of their lives and of making an authentic theology.

The fifth model forms "Christian humanists" who are filled with confidence about the intelligibility of a world created and inhabited by God and about their ability to decipher it. These women and men meditate, like other Christians, on scripture and the tradition which brings it to them. They are looking for something else, however, than they were at the other stages of their development. If they question Christian sources about morals, for example, they do not expect to find a code of Christian behaviour. They are looking for a discourse *(logos)* on biblical or evangelical values *(axios),* an "axiology" typical of Christian conduct. Conscious of being "endowed with intelligence, freewill and autonomous power," as Thomas writes in the prologue of the ethical section of the *Summa,* these individuals recognize that their task is to elaborate an ethics that takes into account the sources of Revelation.

The development of humanist ethics favours the image of a Logos–divinity, guaranteeing the intelligibility of the cosmic and human orders. Word, Light, Subsisting Being, Pure Act, Providence — all are divine names which translate this aspect of the dignity of God. Evidently, these names, like all the others attributed to the divinity, are subject to interpretation. Thus it is with the word "providence." By providence the Stoics meant a rationality intrinsic to the universe that irremediably orients it towards its destiny. Christian writers baptized this Greek notion and attributed it to the Divine Word who is governing the world. All, however, did not understand it in the same way.

Some, who were followers of a legalist ethics, saw a legislating Providence issuing a universal code and choosing some ministers to interpret it. Followers of a humanist ethics thought, rather, of a wise Providence who creates free and reasonable beings to be associated with him in the work of governing the world.

"All that we know of the divine will in our regard," writes Thomas on the issue of our participation as rational creatures in moral discernment, "is that what He wills is our good. By willing the good, our will is then in conformity with the will of God."[30] Since the cosmic order is the work of the creator, all that right reason discerns as the good conforms to the ordinance of the divine logos.

---

[30] *Ibid.*, Ia–IIae, Q. 19, art. 10, ad 1.

Chapter Six

# Stage of Integrity
# and
# Ethics of Response

## Last Transition

Today, Kohlbergian researchers no longer retain stage 6 in the development of human meaning–making. Why have they dropped this second pole of the postconventional level? They claim that the moral protocols they have scored do not furnish sufficient data to prove the existence of a structure of moral reasoning that is distinct from the fifth form. Moreover, to illustrate their sixth stage, Kohlberg and Fowler turned to hagiography. You find in their works the names of contemporary saints such as Gandhi, Martin Luther King, Jr., Dietrich Bonhoeffer, Dag Hammarskjold, Abraham Heschel and Thomas Merton.[1] Others could be

---

[1] L. Kohlberg, C. Levine and A. Hewer, *Moral Stages* (Basel: S. Karger, 1983), pp. 60–64.

added to the list. These individuals have been spontaneously canonized by human communities who recognize them as particularly successful realizations of our common humanity.

Though popular heroes are rare, a relatively impressive number of persons is probably involved in this last evolutionary transition. They already drink of that water which, as Jesus said to the Samaritan woman, "will turn into a spring inside [them] welling up to eternal life" (John 4:14). These people are usually "middle–aged": adults between the interindividual age, when it is thought that the world can be mastered by rational interaction with one's peers, and the final age turned towards death, the irrational event *par excellence* in the life of women and men of all times and cultures. People between these two ages may not manage to pull out of the stage 5 truce before the very act of dying when they accept the renunciations which this withdrawal from stage 5 imposes on them. The restructuration of stage 5 has cost them so much social, cognitive, psychodynamic and moral labour! However, the adult experience of middle age gives them a glimpse, as "in a mirror, darkly" (1 Corinthians 13:12), of what this decisive passage, which would allow them to contemplate their own deaths with serenity, would be like.

These are the elements of the ultimate reversal of spirit (*metanoia*) that we have tried to glean from the reflections of the researchers we have studied. In the less accessible launching zone of the last stage, we admit that the interpretation of human phenomena is more difficult and more than ever influenced by the insights of the interpreter.

## Test of the Reality of Others

One would think that the resolution of the crisis of institutionalism by the structuring of an interindividual self would have definitely resolved the central problem of otherness in human existence. Stage 5 adults have learned, in effect, to recognize both their originality and their interdependence. They can form authentic mutual relationships with others. Do they, however, fully appreciate the unfathomable reality of others?

Take the case of Professor "Jones." In the privacy of his home, he can nourish the illusion that his wife, while becoming herself, has evolved in what he considers the "rather large" frame of his own ideas. His son, according to him, will *obviously* choose the career that attracts him. But then, one fine day, his wife decides to enter the business world. In a short time, she has had more success than he has ever enjoyed. To add insult to injury, she resumes her maiden name, often is away on "business trips," and is excited by a world about which he knows nothing whatsoever. His wife's evolution does not conform at all to the rational projections that the professor made at the interindividual age. While he is still struggling with the overturning of his calculations for the future, he learns that his young adult son wants to be a truck driver, an occupation that does not fit the father's notion of a "career." The manoeuvres of his colleagues at work, of his students, his political partners, and his coreligionists only increase the confusion provoked by the unforeseen paths pursued by his wife and his son.

Things are no different on the wife's side. Her husband, who was so enterprising only yesterday, has suddenly lost his confidence and his energy. Just when her desire has reached its peak, her husband is less and less interested in sexual romps; when she does succeed in stimulating his desire, he no longer has the erectile and orgasmic power of the old days.[2] She is upset: do these peripheral phenomena indicate a general decline of energy? She is mystified, too, by the fact that this man she thought she knew has begun to return to the male subculture he frequented in his adolescence and from which she is excluded.[3] While she is struggling with these changes in her conjugal relations, this woman, whose ambitions and feminism have assumed new proportions, learns that her daughter is abandoning her university studies to become a member of a religious congregation, the Little Sisters of the Poor.

Those whom adults think they know resist them with an unexpected firmness. This new experience of otherness provokes what Fowler discerningly names a "radical relativization of the self as centre." The others are definitely not pieces on a chessboard which individuals have mastered and on which they have imposed a rational strategy. Their own Dream is not shared by others to the degree and in the ways they thought. Between 40 and 60 years of age, a period which Daniel Levinson labels "middle adulthood," individuals must radically modify the shape of the Dream in accord with the "real reality" of others.[4] Levinson evokes here the Jungian notion of "ego deflation." These men undertake to draw a new geographical map in which

---

[2]    E. M. Brecher, *Love, Sex, and Aging: A Consumers Union Report* (New York: Dell, 1976).

[3]    L. Tiger, *Men in Groups* (London: Nelson, 1969).

[4]    D. J. Levinson, *The Seasons of a Man's Life* (New York: Ballantine, 1978). See especially pp. 245–251.

their self occupies a more limited territory. Their new consciousness allows them to glimpse now and then that the centre is everywhere and not just in them. It is not even in an existence that will flower only in the distant future of the Dream.

The secret of human existence does not reside, then, as stage 5 individuals were inclined to think, in a future sublimation of the self. This vision comes from a rationalist dualism which tends to despise the present opacity of embodied individuals in favour of less human but more comprehensible abstractions. On the edge of stage 6, people are ready to free sexuality from the exclusively genital orientation to which they reduced it by their complete preoccupation with rationally ordering their world. They existentially grasp that entering into an intimate sexual rapport with all things corresponds to the aim of the universe. The luxuriance of communion in being surpasses anything their imagination, impoverished by an exclusively rationalist control, ever suspected. No one, in my opinion, has grasped this better than Norman O. Brown, and no one has made a finer analysis of this autumnal metamorphosis of the body of the lover of Being.[5] In the last stage, people have finally developed a "capacity for radical empathy."[6]

In the wonder that the brightness of each creature awakens in them, people finally take the infinitude and totality of Being as the true measure of their own finitude and particularity. By opening a third eye in the middle of the forehead, Hindu tantrism symbolizes the rapture of this

---

[5]  N. O. Brown, *Love's Body* (New York: Random House, 1966).

[6]  S. Keen, *The Passionate Life* (San Francisco: Harper & Row, 1983), p. 202.

new holistic vision of things. A radical confidence in the other becomes possible which enables people to surrender themselves sufficiently, to use a term dear to John Henry Newman, to be able to welcome the other's gift of being.

## Beyond Systematization to Mystery

Meta–ethical questioning has opened stage 5 adults to the intellectual grasp of aspects of human existence more enlightening than what was revealed by the earlier, logical line of reasoning. At the same time that their range of tolerance for other legitimate and reasonable points of view has expanded, their own certitudes have formed around a cognitive process large enough to make space for a multiplicity of systems in dialectical tension. Their rationality has become "universal." It enables them to enter into dialogue with a reasonable and reasoning humanity.

If middle–aged individuals continue to evolve in the cognitive area, they do not do so by completing the task of universalizing their rational thinking process. In this area, as in the area of social interaction, reflection on their long experience obliges them to confront two constant setbacks. On the one hand, the more intellectually honest people join in the collective effort to know the world better, the more they are forced to realize that it is impossible to establish "real proof" for most human affirmations. As early as the master's level, intelligent, young university researchers discover that most "scientific results," published in even the most prestigious journals, are based on experiments that no other researcher can duplicate nor, consequently, verify. These young researchers have not, however, lived long enough to grasp the larger implications of their scientific disappointment. Some day, perhaps, they will have the courage to admit without anxiety that we conduct the whole of our lives on the basis of hypotheses rather than on controlled facts. On the other hand, thoughtful people realize that the best established results of rational discourse always rest, in the last analysis, on presuppositions which are not under the control of the argumentation of reason. Every proof rests on a profession of faith in someone or something, even if it be only human reason.

The assiduous and respectful exercise of reason leads humans to recognize the extent of their ignorance. The more they act according to what distinguishes their animality from that of other mammals, as Aristotle puts it, the more they realize that reason will never resolve the great existential enigmas within it. They come, finally, to a *docta ignorantia.* The wise ignorance of those who have used right reason to grasp its astounding finitude does not lead them to stop reasoning. Nor is this ability to rationalize lost in the course of the ulterior transitions. It is maintained like the other evolutionary acquisitions. However, in the new cognitive pattern of stage 6, it occupies another place and takes on another meaning.

At the end of middle age, individuals are led to the ultimate *metanoia,* which goes beyond and embraces *(meta)* the previous spirit *(noos).* It involves nothing less than replacing the very basis of their certitudes: it is no longer a rational, pretentiously universalizable systematization, but a sharing in the transcendent actuality of Being, this Being whose intentionality is omnipresent, this Being in whose interior all that is persists in existence with unity, truth, goodness and beauty. This intellectual change-over is never the result of something learned in school, not even in the academy of the most illustrious philosophers. Young intellectuals can, certainly, beat everyone else at reciting all the theses with their respective corollaries. But these theses will become neither unshakeable certitudes nor lights shining in their darkness until, by diligent use of human reason, these young people realize how feeble is the knowledge they distil.

"Hogwash!" protest scientific spirits whose practice of science has not yet taught them humility. How do we answer them? Situated as it is below this level of perception, rational argumentation will never succeed in elaborating proof of what is beyond its ken. Rational spirits, whose lot it is to explain "the facts" should, however, explain the following fact: from where does the lucidity and unshakeable certitude of the sages come? Their light and their internal conviction do not depend on the coherence of universal reasoning. These sages, moreover, never reflect on the basis of systematic abstractions. They do not explain the particular by the universal. On the contrary, it is precisely the quality of their knowledge of concrete and singular realities which makes them visionaries of eternity. The most everyday realities — a flower, a child, a stream of water, a crowd — are inexhaustible sources of wonder for them. The world of symbols, as James Fowler very pertinently notes, has become transparent. "Stage 6 persons are profound shapers and regenerators of symbols, due to the immediate quality of their relation to and participation in transcendent actuality."[7]

---

[7]    J. W. Fowler, "Life/Faith Patterns," in J. Berryman (ed.), *Life Maps* (Waco: Winston Press, 1978), p. 90.

## Integral Self

The nonagenarian Erik Erikson confided to Daniel Goleman of *The New York Times* in June 1988: "You have to learn to accept life's law and face the fact that we will slowly disintegrate."[8] This, no doubt, is the most convincing experience of finitude through which most middle–aged adults are called upon to live. Unless individuals between 40 and 60 years of age pathologically refuse to face reality, they can no longer read the signs of their human vulnerability as simple accidents along the way. The slogans that invite us to "think young" and that try to convince us that growing old is the consequence of a defeatist psychology are nonsense. No middle–aged adult can sincerely believe in them. As Erikson notes, these slogans contradict a fundamental law of biological life. Living organisms, with everything they have built to adapt to their life milieu, last for the time allotted them and then waste away.

Erikson, reflecting on this experience of the adult age and its psychodynamic implications, has described an old age in the course of which individuals should have acquired enough confidence in their own sense of completion to ward off the despair provoked by physical disintegration and the nearness of death it portends. Erikson describes the last task as integrity versus despair. The victorious feeling of wholeness, completeness, totality and personal plenitude is the fruit of each individual accepting, without bitterness, his or her unique cycle of life. It is not that they feel they are better than other people! Rather, they see themselves as a valid and precious version of the human being, an

---

[8] *The New York Times,* June 14, 1988, p. Y 13.

authentic participation in Being. Fear of death no longer reigns when one has no regrets.

Consequently, identity in old age is not shaped by regrets for what might have been in the past, nor, obviously, by hope for changes in the future. It is redefined in terms of present reality. It is structured in relation to the Absolute which solicits attention, respect and care in the smallest things. People with an integrated self are content to eat when they eat, to sleep when they sleep, to recreate when they recreate, and to work when they work. If they are reconciled to "what is," ordinary though it be, this is because they have fully acquired the existential certitude that there is nothing other than what is. Beyond authentic presence to the being of things and people, there is only illusion.

Old age's virtue, according to Erikson, is what has traditionally been called wisdom. He defines it simply as a detached preoccupation with life itself in the face of death.

## Moral Metanomy

*Meta* comes from the Greek and indicates succession (that which comes after), beyond (that which is higher), and participation (that which includes). "Metanomy" must not be confused with "anomie" (without law) nor "antinomian" (against law). I intend to use the word to indicate going beyond the moral law in which one participates.

According to Kohlberg, the sixth stage of morality is never anything more than an extension of the universalizing ability of reasoning which goes to work when access to the postconventional level is gained. In my opinion, this conception does not satisfactorily explain the over–all human development we have just described. The latest Kohlbergian reflections suggest, moreover, that we should, perhaps, look in another direction. On the one hand, the Harvard Center for Moral Education has dropped stage 6 "as a commonly identifiable form of moral reasoning."[9] On the other hand, Kohlberg himself speculated, from the mid–seventies, on a subsequent stage "in a faith perspective."[10]

Basing themselves on interviews of elderly persons conducted by Fowler, Kohlberg and some of his associates suggested a stage 7 in which development culminates in a holistic sense of participation in the cosmic order. Whether it has theistic, pantheistic or agnostic connotations, this sense of participation provides an ultimate foundation for normative moral principles. Kohlberg insisted, however, that this kind of ethical–religious thinking goes beyond reasoning based on postconventional-level principles of justice. This concept was hard for the research tool he had developed to grasp.

It seems that the hunch Kohlberg had in middle age, that there was a supra–rational form of judgment, is correct. Nonetheless, I think that his interpretation still owes too much to rationalism. The "cosmic identity" he evokes never goes beyond the idea of a natural law assuring the order of the world. However, the crisis of middle age does not, I think, pull moral development in the direction of a more and more acute sense of the validity of the order of right

---

[9]   L. Kohlberg, C. Levine, and A. Hewer, *Moral Stages,* p. 60.

[10]   L. Kohlberg, "Education, Moral Development and Faith," *Journal of Moral Education,* Vol. 4, 1974, pp.. 5–16; F. C. Power and L. Kohlberg, "Religion, Morality, and Ego Development," in C. Brusselmans and others, *Toward Moral and Religious Maturity* (Morristown: Silver Burdett, 1980), pp. 344–372.

reason, which is involved in judging the best means to take to guarantee the humanization of human relations. When people leave the interindividual truce, they become aware that, right though they may be, the most rational moral judgments will never succeed in universally establishing liberty, equality and fraternity.

To the degree that stage 5 has been a success, people at stage 6 still know how to practise the art of the rational discernment of good and evil. Consequently, in the moral decisions that they have to make or evaluate, they still strive to rationally discern just judgments from those that are unjust. But what has characterized their evolution since stage 5 is their experience of the finitude of every creature and of his or her deliberations. Experience has also taught them that not even the most rational discernment necessarily wins the assent and the moral commitment of the free subjects that we are. Above all, they recognize that every moral decision is radically arbitrary.

A decision is "arbitrary" when it is made by an "arbiter" (referee or judge) on the basis of free will *(liberum arbitrium)* alone, and not on the basis of obedience to rules. An arbitrary decision proceeds from a freedom to interpret and to act. It escapes the determinism of compelling evidence and rationalist pretensions of "scientific expertise." Depending on the quality of the will, the moral decision will be, then, either a vulgar product of geometry and covetousness or a creation of delicacy and generosity. At the stage of moral metanomy, discernment and commitment are exercised on the basis of principles that depend on a certitude of a completely different order than rational links of causality. Empirical research, which is the product of western rationalism, has not yet succeeded in determining either its origin or its nature.

## Response Model

In 1950, sociologist David Riesman reduced the ethical social models to three: traditional–directed types, inner–directed types and other–directed types.[11] In 1959, philosopher Jean Lacroix stated that there are three levels of moral experience: duty, value, and freedom and love.[12] In 1963, theologian Richard Niebuhr described three ethical models: the deontological model of *homo civilis,* the teleological model of *homo faber,* and the relational model of *homo dialogus.*[13] In 1967, historian Edward Long discovered three motifs in Christian ethics: prescriptive, deliberative and relational.[14] In 1979, ethicist James Nelson wrote that there are three styles of the decisional process in morals: obedience, aspiration and response.[15]

Each of these authors is saying, in his own way, what most of his colleagues are also thinking. All undertake to describe and analyse the elements of the last in their list, that which I have named the response model. Current research gives rise to a plethora of systems of thought that

---

[11]  D. Riesman, *The Lonely Crowd* (New Haven: Yale University Press, 1950).

[12]  J. Lacroix, *Le sens de l'athéisme moderne* 2nd. ed., (Tournai: Casterman, 1959), p. 96.

[13]  H. R. Niebuhr, *The Responsible Self: An Essay in Christian Moral Philosophy* (New York: Harper & Row, 1963).

[14]  E. L. Long, *A Survey of Christian Ethics* (New York: Oxford University Press, 1967).

[15]  J. B. Nelson, *Embodiment: An Approach to Sexuality and Christian Theology* (Minneapolis: Augsburg, 1979), p. 119–120.

differ greatly one from the other. I do not know of any, however, that has managed to serve as a point of reference outside the small circles of specialists. I do, nonetheless, find common positions in most of these systems. They thematize moral experience around the idea of an altruistic, realistic and communitarian response. We shall briefly examine these three aspects of a model which fits the experience of the moral metanomy of stage 6.

In the sixth model, the moral project is thought of as an agent's wholehearted response to the beckoning presence of others. In the beginning is the Other who, solely by being present to me, calls me. To live in freedom, the Other asks of me nothing less than the gift of my actualizing presence. This altruistic response was expressed by the ancients in the notion of benevolence: love which *wills* his or her *good* to the other. The basic appetency of this love is that the other fully be what he or she is in the presence of the lover. The altruistic response thus restores an economy of pure gratuity in which beings accept one another in their freedom to be.[16] In this model, otherness no longer functions principally through a relationship of pleasure, self–interest, fusion, authority or justice; otherness is, rather, established through a relationship of generous reciprocity.

In this response model, the golden rule also works differently than it did in the preceding models.[17] It is neither a rule of survival and reprisal nor a principle of eternal and

---

[16]  J.–C. Sagne, *Conflit, changement, conversion: Vers une éthique de la réciprocité* (Paris: Cerf, 1974); V. P. Furnish, *The Love Commandment in the New Testament* (Nashville: Abingdon Press, 1972).

[17]  O. Du Roy, *La réciprocité: Essai de morale fondamentale* (Paris: Épi, 1970), pp. 31–49.

internal order. The "always treat others as you would like to be treated" idea of the Golden Rule as we find it expressed, for example, in Matthew 7:12, expresses nothing less than the weight that generous love has as the ultimate measure in the taking of any moral decision. In the *Confessions,* Augustine expresses this first principle of ethics in one of the most famous maxims of moral wisdom: *Pondus meum, amor meus.*[18]

When love is the measure of the response to the solicitations of others, human relations are lived in a time qualitatively different from the *krônos* measured by watches and chronometers. The time of love is something other than that of justice. This latter, chronologically, flows indifferently for all, in instants of the same duration and the same value. Many gospel parables, and most notably the parable of the workers sent into the vineyard (Matthew 20:1–16), teach us two ways to measure time. The first is a rationalist equity which, in order to reach universalizable decisions, must not be preoccupied with the rhythms proper to each person. The second is altruistic love. This, on the contrary, needs a time in relation to the historical becoming of the other. Personal moments do not all have the same value. There is a certain complicity of personal events and dispositions which make it happen that, at this subjective phase of a life story, the time is favourable for action. Theologians have baptized this existential time, *kairos.* It means "good timing," the opportune time that only love can detect. The sense of *kairos* gives ethical responses that assured discretion, that finesse of execution, and that

---

[18]    Augustine, *Confessions,* Bk. 13, c. 10, translated by J. K. Ryan (Garden City: Images Books, 1960), p. 341.

rightness of feeling that are missing from the decisions and commitments governed by universalizing reason.

Since it is the product of generous love, the response of this last ethical model seeks to be attentive not only to others and their existential rhythm, but to all the realities in which it should be inserted. It is a realistic response, given by a "respons–able" agent, that is to say, someone able to produce a response well suited to the precise context.[19] This characteristic is so significant that this ethics is often called "contextual" or "situation" ethics. It distrusts the deductive methods of the preceding model because it proceeds from a concept of the ideal human that is often *a priori*. Without denying the important insights and dreams of earlier days, individuals with an ethics of response tend to favour the inductive approach. Even values and principles are constantly submitted to the test of experimental knowledge because so many of them, in fact, have turned out to be prejudiced and prejudicial! Its approach, then, is more operational. Questions of conduct are not posed in abstract terms but, preferably, in terms of, and in reference to, what is going on. The agents think that the task of moral discernment is to accomplish what is presently and contextually possible. They know from experience that the best is, effectively, the enemy of the good.

The loving and realistic response of the last ethical model also embraces the community. It sees people continually being born and reborn out of their reciprocal relationships of love. It is only in sharing community, as

---

[19] On this ethical realism, see R. O. Johann, *Building the Human* (New York: Herder and Herder, 1968), pp. 117–188; D. C. Maguire, *The Moral Choice* (Garden City: Doubleday, 1978), pp. 71–75.

Emmanuel Mounier and the whole personalist school saw very well, that people thus are humanized.[20] This, moreover, is an old idea of Greek ethics that we have too long neglected. It labels anyone who tries to confine love to the private domain an idiot (*idiotes:* the purely particular). This oversimplifying of spirit, this ineptitude comes from a dualistic refusal of incorporation that tries to separate the self from the body politic. Those who do this deprive love of its power to defend its freedom of action.

Many consequences for the elaboration of a good moral decision flow from this third fundamental position. First, a moral decision is taken only in terms of a specific sociocultural *locus* which helps to shape the facts and the interpretations. Next, it calls for attention to a possible community consensus on the concrete configuration of values on which the communication of social friendship is founded. Nevertheless, it does not expect a pluralistic world to yield a uniform, *a priori* agreement on ends and values. The agents have experienced reality and the enrichment that difference brings to it. In the community dialogue they are looking, then, for sufficient agreement on common, practical actions. They are convinced that, through concrete actions, the meaning of existence rises up, defines itself and opens new paths to love. Finally, this decision-making process considers the most widespread moral evil to be the passive tolerance of a dehumanizing social state that one could help to change.

---

[20]   E. Mounier, *Personalism* (London: Routledge and Kegan Paul, 1952).

## Presence to Ultimate Realities

Too often the spontaneous reaction of many moral people is to prepare a community of love for the future rather than to respond lovingly to the invitation addressed to them in the humble circumstances of daily life. Since they are too busy solving middle- and long-term problems, they neglect the most obvious and radical problem: the quality of their presence to others. At the heart of the response model is the basic insight that our moral history is not something separate on the periphery of everyday life where, we often feel, nothing much is really happening. The response ethics prompts us to leave this parallel history aside and to enter directly into the history unfolding before our eyes. An ethics of the everyday, of the now, it favours concrete realizations rather than speculation. Agents do not create morality until their reassuring presence helps a battered child smile at life once again or they listen to the tales of some old woman who has no one else to whom "to say herself." For them, the good is nowhere other than in that child's smile or this old woman's quite literal "self–expression." Beyond concrete persons who have a zest for life, moral good does not exist. This is why the Lord is recognized only in the starving who are fed, the thirsty who are given drink, the strangers who are welcomed, the naked who are clothed, the sick and the imprisoned who are visited (Matthew 25:31–46).

Friedrich Schleiermacher advises us to do all *with* religion, but nothing *because of* religion. People who live the response model do all that they do with a moral inspiration but nothing because of moral obligation. Why? Because moral obligation arises out of a perception of a gap between what is and what should be. To the degree that there is no longer a perception of a gap to be spanned, moral obligation disappears. In Paradise, whether in the myth of the beginning or in the myth of the end–time, morality does not exist. Just as vision replaces faith and love hope, so wisdom replaces morality.

To the degree that people in their last years regain a "second innocence" or the simplicity they had before conscience split into "I" and "self,"[21] they become present to Reality in the way they were during their childhood. This second time, however, they are present as individuals fully differentiated from all that is other. They have no further need of symbolic mediations (institutions, laws, rituals, doctrine, morality, sacraments). Moreover, as Paul teaches the Romans (see Romans 7), the presence of the moral good itself frees them from the moral law. In the presence of "that which is," the rapture and the exultation of love take the place of the moral project of "what ought to be."

Need we add that this situation describes the threshold of the blessed life, where evil loses its power? People who reach this stage are so reconciled to their creaturely finitude and sinfulness that no criticism or setback can get through to them. They are finally ready to welcome, with pure thanksgiving, the gift of life in its fullness.

## Oversimplifying Imitations

The grandeur of response ethics constitutes, unfortunately, its weakness. This ethics does not function well except for those who actually have reached the stage of moral metanomy. Sam Keen terms the idea of teaching young

---

[21]  V. Jankélévitch, *Traité des vertus* (Paris: Bordas, 1970), Vol. 2, pp. 503–514.

people holiness, and catechetical answers about love, ridiculous. They have not really sinned yet; they have not, then, discovered how deep is their mistrust.[22] From this point of view, we must acknowledge the ambiguity of canonizing young "saints." That Maria Goretti succeeded in fighting off the sexual advances of her attacker, and that she had been a well–behaved young lady otherwise, does not tell much about the "weight of love" that enlightened her discernments. But it is this weight alone, according to Paul (1 Corinthians 13), that has eternal value.

Consequently, ethical systems which, like that advanced by Joseph Fletcher,[23] reduce moral discernment to the magic formula, "Do the most loving thing in each situation," are severely criticized by most ethicists. We should be just as sceptical of little *agapé* groups that believe they can change the world by holding tight to one another while singing hymns and exchanging life stories. In order for moral and meta–moral discernments to reach their perfection under the weight of love, agents must have been purified in the crucible of the evolution of meaning–making and carry in them a wisdom that continually adjusts them, connaturally, to its objects. Until they come to this state, love is too blind to resolve accurately the complex questions with which we are confronted. The Augustinian command "to love and do what you will" works for lovers of Augustine's stature.

---

[22]  S. Keen, "Body/Faith: Trust, Dissolution and Grace," in J. Berryman (ed.), *Life Maps* (Waco: Winston Press, 1978), p. 123.

[23]  J. F. Fletcher, *Situation Ethics: The New Morality* (Philadelphia: Westminster Press, 1966).

Because the imitators of love sin by oversimplifying in their assessment of the exigencies of an altruistic response, their realism degenerates into a flat, anti–intellectual pragmatism. They ignore all the attentive respect, eloquent silence and wonder–filled contemplation which characterizes a loving presence. Their ethics is more closely related to hedonism or utilitarianism than to an ethics of response.

The imitators of this last model also betray themselves by their inability to give an authentic community response. In order to will the good of the human community effectively, one must humbly insert oneself in it and espouse its concrete values and preoccupations. Freud wanted to be spared a love that pretends to save others despite themselves.[24] Real lovers, who love with an authentic, redeeming love, neither think nor behave like "colonial missionaries." Jesus pitched his tent in a specific corner of a country and practised his trade in the midst of his people. If his loving words succeeded in reaching the whole human community, it is because they were really addressed to the "local folks." Nothing has universal appeal unless it makes sense of the particular.

## Religious Testimony and the Liberating God

In one of the finest documents issued by the modern papal magisterium, the *Apostolic Exhortation on Evangelization,* Paul VI writes, "Modern man listens more willingly

---

[24]  S. Freud, "Civilization and Its Discontents," in J. Strachey (ed.), *The Standard Edition of the Complete Psychological Works of Sigmund Freud* (London: Hogarth Press and the Institute of Psycho–analysis, 1953–1966), Vol. XXI, pp. 108–116.

to witnesses than to teachers, and if he does listen to teachers, it is because they are witnesses."[25] The religiously
credible person is someone who transcends formulas and
creeds and is in communion with the divine reality. John,
the disciple loved above all others, offered his readers no
other credentials than the authenticity of his witness:
"Something . . . we have heard, that we have seen with our
own eyes; that we have watched and touched with our
hands: the Word, who is life . . . we saw it and we are giving
our testimony" (1 John 1:1–2). The lover standing in his or
her truth in the presence of the Beloved cannot lie.

Christians at stage 6 no longer search scripture and tradition for consoling or inspirational pieties, for recipes of
salvation, ready–made answers or blueprints. They meditate on the historical witness that is offered by those sincere
men and women who, while they were constructing their
world through a loving interaction with others, progressively discovered the real face of the Living God through
faith. The solutions of "this crowd of witnesses" (Hebrews
12:1) are neither eternal nor unchangeable; some of their
values are not necessarily ours. What is always current is
the progressive discovery of God by faith through a loving
and liberating practice of humanity.[26]

The moral experience of response disposes believers to
escape, finally, from those divinities the Old Testament
called idols. These idols are the deceitful reflections of

---

[25]   *Origins,* Vol. 5, 1976, p. 464.

[26]   G. Bonnet, *Au nom de la bible et de l'évangile, quelle morale?*
(Paris: Le Centurion, 1978). See also, with more insistance on the community aspect, J. Murphy–O'Connor, *Becoming Human Together* (Wilmington: M. Glazier, 1977), particularly pp. 147–237.

sameness, the things known to which we still cling so tightly that we cannot jettison them and bring ourselves fully to
birth. Unlike the idols, the Living God is the epiphany in
our world of the liberating Difference. God manifests himself to those who love him as the Wholly Other who, by the
gratuitousness of his presence, delivers them to themselves.

As long as the liberating experience of unconditional
love has not brought to an end the evolutionary process by
which subjects expel all that is not themselves from the side
of otherness (the object), God cannot be perceived as
Wholly Other. As long as the divine is not wholly other, it
does not allow us to be wholly ourselves. As Walter Kasper
writes: "It is precisely when God is taken seriously as God
that he liberates the world to be the world."[27] From this
comes the pseudo–problem of the competition between
God and his creature that haunted theology from Pelagius
to the Reformers. While Pelagius made himself the spokesperson for those who claimed to save the creature and his
or her free initiative, Calvin came to the defence of God and
his predestination. The two presuppose that attributing too
much dignity to one lessens the dignity of the other. The
practice of a response ethics exposes the pettiness of this
presupposition.

Taking seriously the otherness of the gratuitous God of
Jesus Christ, as Claude Ortemann's marvellous little book
calls him,[28] is not the product of pure reflection, not even
of a reflection directed by faith. Only a loving praxis enables the discovery of a God who, in Jesus Christ,

---

[27] W. Kasper, *The God of Jesus Christ* (New York: Crossroad,
1984), p. 26.

[28] *Le Dieu gratuit de Jésus Christ* (Paris: Desclée, 1986).

gratuitously offers the poor, the voiceless and the marginalized a love that frees them from their fear to be themselves. That is also what we read in Matthew's gospel (25:31–46): the traits of the liberating God can be discerned only in the exercise of a generosity that gives others the gift of life.

# Conclusion

Is our new knowledge about the stages of moral development likely to enrich that art of arts — the humanizing conduct of our lives?

This new knowledge greatly affects the methods of moral education. First, knowledge of the stages invites us to pay more attention to the structural development of the young than to their moral indoctrination. Development of the forms of discernment and moral commitment seems to be much more decisive for the spiritual evolution of a person than the transmission of moral codes. Secondly, knowledge of the stages allows us to discern more clearly the moral and religious values that the young are capable of discovering in the successive phases of their moral development. Consequently, the discovery of the stages has opened up a vast area of pedagogical research in moral education.

This new knowledge also has repercussions for our own adult lives. Lawrence Kohlberg has underlined two essential aspects of proper usage of the sequence of moral development. The existential and practical import of these remarks has been lost in the academic context in which they were uttered.

The first point concerns the attitude we should adopt towards the other in the ethical debates which are assuming more and more importance in our pluralistic society. Kohlberg warns us about making moral judgments about people on the basis of the stage at which they make discernments. On the one hand, the stage tells us nothing about the good or evil content of their discernments and moral acts. People at stage 2 are just as capable of "doing good and avoiding evil" or, on the contrary, of "doing evil and avoiding the good" as those at stage 5. On the other hand, the free play of liberty in moral development escapes our examination and judgment. The attention we should give to the phenomenon of moral development helps us to understand and to put into practice Paul's exacting command that we not judge others (Romans 2:1–2). In our dealings with others, the developmental sequence decodes the meanings of their moral discernments. Once we have grasped the internal logic of another's meaning–making, we can identify the profound sources of disagreement and enter into a more constructive dialogue.

The second point concerns the nature of our own moral task. By showing that the stages represent a qualitative progression, Kohlberg affirms the normativity of the sequence itself.[1] This means that the sequence of the stages of development is a value to pursue. This implies neither that people who reach the higher stages make fewer mistakes in

---

[1]     L. Kohlberg, "The Claim to Moral Adequacy of a Highest Stage of Moral Judgment," *The Journal of Philosophy,* Vol. 70, 1973, pp. 630–646.

their judgments or moral commitments, nor that they make more good moral choices. At every level you can find virtuous and dissolute people. However, once the limitations of Kohlberg's affirmations have been made clear, we must acknowledge that an action that flows from a discernment at the first level is not of the same quality as one that flows from a discernment at the second or third level. Since they proceed from subjects who are more clearly differentiated from their objects, the human quality of judgment and moral commitment improves at each higher level. Underlying every educational undertaking is the admission that increased knowledge, a developed personality and a well–practised sociability improve behaviour.

Although we admit that this position is correct in relation to education in general, we have not sufficiently appreciated its importance in the area of morals. We restrict the area of moral responsibility to the good or evil content of each moral decision: telling the truth or lying, protecting the environment or polluting it, respecting the intimacy of children or abusing one's power over them. More fundamental and important is the responsibility we have to discern what paths our moral development is taking and to commit ourselves courageously to the arduous tasks, the painful uprootings and agonizing risks implied in every evolutionary transition. Perhaps we shall understand better the meaning of the gospel call to *metanoia*. The reversal of our spirit and the changing of our heart matter more than this good deed or that fault. It is a question of the very quality of all our responses to the presence of the Other.

The sequence of moral development, in fact, represents the process of decentration subjects go through. By jettisoning the successive identities they have borrowed, subjects are gradually born to themselves and grow in their humanity. To the degree that they let go of their illusory identifications, subjects leave others the space they need to show themselves in their authentic otherness. For example, for those who became active members of society by abandoning the reassuring fusional attachments of stage 3, relationships at stage 4 take on a new quality of justice. These place others before them as autonomous persons with rights. At stage 5, subjects tear open the institutional envelope of the self by discovering the rational foundation of their dignity as persons. In the other they meet more than a fellow citizen: they meet a person with whom they share the same humanity. The legal normativity which taints all moral behaviour with rigidity and coldness gives way to the finesse of prudential deliberation. This is the only way to invent responses that are perfectly adjusted to the human contexts which provoke them. Individuals progressively purified by the inexhaustible mystery of otherness are ready, at stage 6, to cast off the last lines of an overly rationalist reason. Their relationships with others are finally lived in the economy of a welcoming presence and free responses which testify to a freedom that has finally been consumed in love.

The traditional moral teaching about the fundamental option, the paths of spiritual progress, growth in virtue, etc., show that the idea of moral development is not something new in ethical thinking. The constructivist school's contemporary research on the stages of development helps to understand better the successive forms of our quest for meaning and human integrity.

# Bibliography

## On the work of Jean Piaget:

– Boyle, D.G. *A Student's Guide to Piaget*. Oxford: Pergamon, 1969.

– Campbell, S.F., ed. *Piaget Sampler: An Introduction to Jean Piaget Through His Own Words*. New York: Wiley, 1976.

– Elkind, D. and J.H. Flavell, eds. *Studies in Cognitive Development: Essays in Honor of Jean Piaget*. New York: Oxford University Press, 1969.

– Evans, R.I. et al. *Jean Piaget: The Man and His Ideas*. New York: E.P. Dutton, 1973.

– Ginsburg, H. and S. Opper. *Piaget's Theory of Intellectual Development: An Introduction*. Englewood Cliffs: Prentice-Hall, 1969.

– Piaget, J. "Piaget's Theory," in Musen, P.H. and W. Kessen, eds. *Handbook of Child Psychology*, Vol. I, *History, Theory, and Methods*, 4th ed. New York: John Wiley and Sons, 1983, pp. 103-128.

## On the work of Lawrence Kohlberg:

– Brusselmans, C. et al. *Toward Moral and Religious Maturity: The First International Conference on Moral and Religious Development*. Morristown: Silver Burdett, 1980.

– Duska, R. and M. Whelan. *Moral Development: A Guide to Piaget and Kohlberg*. New York: Paulist Press, 1975.

– Kohlberg, L., C. Levine and A. Hewer. *Moral Stages: A Current Formulation and a Response to Critics*. Basel: S. Karger, 1983.

- Mathias, G.J. *Moral Development and Psychosocial Development: A Comparative Study of the Developmental Theories of Lawrence Kohlberg and Erik H. Erikson.* Rome: Academia Alfonsiana, 1987.

- Modgil, S. and C. Modgil, eds. *Lawrence Kohlberg: Consensus and Controversy.* London: Falmer Press, 1986.

- Munsey, B., ed. *Moral Development, Moral Education, and Kohlberg: Basic Issues in Philosophy, Psychology, Religion, and Education.* Birmingham: Religious Education Press, 1980.

- Purpel, D. and K. Ryan, eds. *Moral Education. It Comes with the Territory.* Berkeley: McCutchan, 1976, pp. 171-307.

- Rest, J.R. "Morality," in Mussen, P.H., J.H. Flavell and E.M. Markman, eds. *Handbook of Child Psychology.* Vol III, *Cognitive Development.* 4th ed. New York: John Wiley and Sons, 1983, pp. 556-629.

- Schrader, D. *The Legacy of Lawrence Kolberg.* San Franscisco: Jossey-Bass, 1990.

## For further reading on ethical theories:

- Bourke, V.J. *History of Ethics.* Garden City: Doubleday, 1968.

- Long, E.L. *A Survey of Christian Ethics.* New York: Oxford University Press, 1967, pp. 45-164.

- Perelman, C. *A Historical Introduction to Philosophical Thinking.* New York: Random House, 1968.

- Plé, A. *Duty or Pleasure? A New Appraisal of Christian Ethics.* New York: Paragon House, 1986.

- Slaatte, H.A. *A Critical Survey of Ethics.* Lanham: University Press of America, 1988.